DIMENSIONS

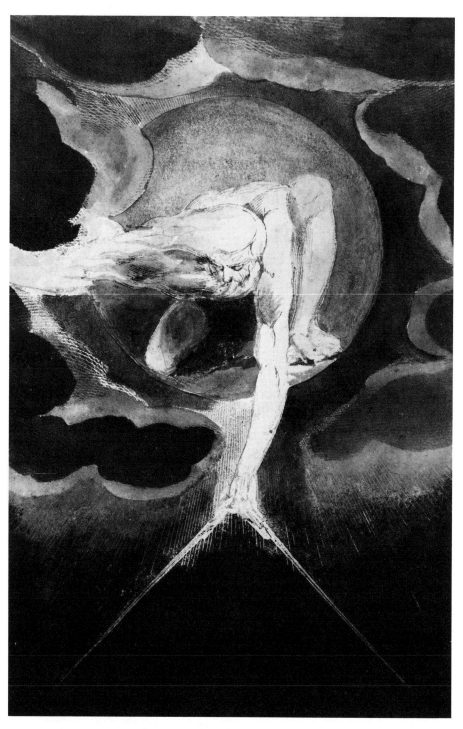

"The Ancient of Days," by William Blake

DIMENSIONS

Space, Shape, & Scale in Architecture

Charles Moore   Gerald Allen

Architectural Record Books, New York

The editors were Hugh S. Donlan
    and Martin Filler.
The designer was Tina Beebe.
Set in Baskerville by Design/Type, Inc.
Printed by Halliday Lithograph Corporation.
Bound by The Book Press.
First Edition

"Two Buildings by Joseph Esherick" began
in different form as an essay in *Architectural
Forum*; "St. Thomas Church," "The
Minneapolis Federal Reserve," "Likenesses,"
"Discrimination in Housing Design," and
"Modesty" as essays in *Architectural Record*;
"Schindler and Richardson" as essays in *The
Journal of the Society of Architectural
Historians* and *Progressive Architecture*;
"Inclusive and Exclusive," "Hadrian's
Villa," and "You Have to Pay for the Public
Life" as essays in *Perspecta: The Yale
Architectural Journal*; and "Southernness"
as an essay in *Perspecta: Yale Papers on
Architecture*.

Published by Architectural Record,
A McGraw-Hill Publication,
1221 Avenue of the Americas,
New York, New York 10020

Moore, Charles Willard, 1925-
    Dimensions: space, shape & scale in architecture.

    Includes bibliographical references and index.
    1. Space (Architecture) 2. Architecture—Compo-
sition, proportion, etc. 3. Visual perception.
4. Harmony (Aesthetics) I. Allen, Gerald, joint author.
II. Title.

NA2765.M66   729   76-28406
ISBN 0-07-002336-0

Contents

Preface

This book is a series of architectural walking tours. The buildings described are from widely different times and places, and they are in the low and middle styles, as well as the high one. They are linked only by the immodestly evident thread of our admiration for them (or, in a few cases where that seemed important, our lack of admiration) and by a small set of general concepts we think are useful in looking not only at them, but at any buildings. These are described in the first four chapters: "Dimensions," "Space," "Shape," and "Scale." These chapters are intended to be simple and concise, and so they may also seem to lack subtlety. We hope that they also seem clear.

Gerald Allen
Charles Moore
New York City, March 1976

Tympanum, by Lee Lawrie, above the main entrance to the RCA Building in New York

Before thir eyes in sudden view appear
The secrets of the hoary deep, a dark
Illimitable Ocean without bound
Without dimension, where length, breadth, and highth,
And time and place are lost; where eldest Night
And Chaos, *Ancestors of Nature, hold*
Eternal Anarchy, amidst the noise
Of endless wars, and by confusion stand.

Milton, Paradise Lost, *Book II*

Dimensions

Dimensions are independent variables, aspects that can increase or decrease without altering any other variable. In geometry we say that a line has only one dimension. A point on the line can be moved to any other place on the line without affecting anything else, and, to the question "Where is it?" there is only one kind of answer: four, five, or a thousand feet from wherever it was to begin with.

A plane is a two-dimensional affair, because any point on it can be described in relation to two points on two lines, or coordinates, at right angles to each other on the plane. The two dimensions are independent, because the point on the plane can, if we choose, be relocated so as to alter only one dimension — by moving it in a straight line parallel to the other dimension.

But we usually think of things as being located in free space, rather than on a line or a plane, and we think of this space as having three dimensions. We think this because we note that it can be measured in three mutually independent directions: up or down, forward or backward, and from one side to the other. There are three, and only three, dimensions by which we can locate a point in free space; any other coordinate we introduce will itself be dependent on the first three.

Nonetheless, the question of dimensions does not at all have to be considered geometrically. We can just as well choose something else — any other quantity we wish to represent. Force, for instance, is a dimension. Take a screen

1

door that has just been snapped shut by a spring. How much can we open it by pulling on the handle? This is a two-dimensional question, for the answer depends on two independent variables: how hard we pull (a force) and how tight the spring is (also a force). Maps are standardly thought of as two-dimensional things. But they easily can, and most often do, have more dimensions than this. If the map is of a city, for example, we can put clusters of dots on it to represent the population density in various neighborhoods, with each dot standing for a certain number of people. We can also make the dots different shapes to signify the ethnic origins of the inhabitants, and we can make clusters of dots different colors to show the density and ethnic makeup of the population at different points in time. The map will then have five dimensions: height and width, plus the number, shape, and color of the dots. These last three are dimensions just like the first two, because they are each variables, and because each can vary without altering any of the others.

Architectural plans always have more than two dimensions. The word *plan* itself suggests these additional variables in its semantic drift from the etymological origin, *plane*, to the more general meaning — an intent, or a course of action. An architect's plan for a house is loaded with symbols and numbers; sometimes it will have colors as well, and always it will have the implicit conventions of drawing — like the *Beaux Arts* habit of relying on the thickness of a wall in plan to express the height of a room, it being assumed that in load-

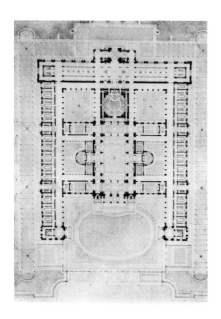

"Un Palais des Sociétés Savantes" (1893), by Paul Dusart, from *Les Grands Prix de Rome, 1850-1900*

bearing masonry buildings the thicker the wall the higher the ceiling. All of these things on the architect's drawing are themselves dimensions, independent variables, just like the dots on the city map. Furthermore, they represent a much more complex host of dimensions in the actual building: the amount of heat needed to boil a kettle of water, the amount of water needed to brush one set of teeth, the amount of force needed to hold the roof up (or keep it on, during a high wind), or the amount, and indeed the kind, of sunlight that will be admitted through so many windows of such and such a size in any particular place. Which brings up an obvious point: architecture has many more than three dimensions.

Architects naturally think of the dimensions of space as being of primary importance to what they are doing, though sometimes the practice of designing two-dimensional plans leads them to go repetitively to the third spatial dimension, resulting in ceilings uniformly eight feet high. But even when they are thinking in three dimensions, they can still trivialize the dimensional problem. Height, width, and depth, which we measure with coordinates X, Y, and Z, are not *the* three dimensions, they are merely *three* dimensions. Even the famous "fourth" dimension, time, is not that, though it can, if we wish be *a* fourth dimension. Since any independent variable can be a dimension, the number of dimensions can be expanded in many directions and is completely arbitrary, depending on what is significant to the problem at hand. The question is this:

3

"What are the variables to be observed?" And the answer is still another question: "What do you care to measure?"

If three dimensions can generate what we standardly think of as space, then all the dimensions the mind can perceive are capable of generating *perceptual spaces*. Perceptual spaces, of course, have none of that sense of "whereness" that we associate with three-dimensional space, or at least with objects located in it. But it is important to remember, in fact, that the sense of "whereness" may well be no more than a convenient habit. As far as we have any way of knowing, three-dimensional space does not exist outside of our minds, and the feelings of height and width and depth — like those of light, sound, color, temperature, smell, or any other perceptible variable — are not objective realities: they are the results of complex neurocomputations in the brain, based on signals from the body's sensory equipment.

Perceptual spaces can have one dimension or many. The number and kind depend alike on cultural conditioning, particular training, and even personal inclination on the part of the beholder. Thus, in a manner that is altogether baffling to most "civilized" peoples, Australian aborigines can understand subtle shifts of sand, Eskimos can understand snow, and primitive tribes along the Amazon can understand the jungle. The latter, because they are unfamiliar with the perception of great depths, are prone to total disorientation when they are taken out into the open, just as the rest of us would be disoriented by being taken in.

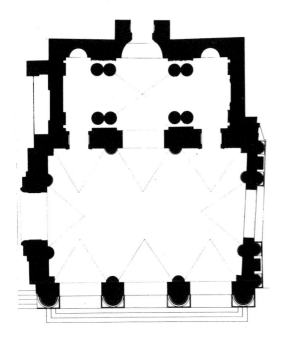

Plan of the Loggia Del Capitaniato (1571), by Andrea Palladio, from *Corpus Palladianum*

By force of their particular training, harbor pilots can sense eddies and currents imperceptible to the uninitiated observer; coffee tasters can judge a nearly infinite combination of kind and quality of beans, and piano tuners can hear the dissonances of the tempered scale that pass for harmonies to most other people. Such perceptions are part of these people's perceptual spaces. All of us, moreover, can understand or misunderstand certain things according to our temporary or permanent inclinations. We hear the alarm that wakes us up in the morning, but not the clock that chimes the hours all night. Some people respond positively to green, others negatively, and still other negatively only when it is in combination with purple. Some people's neurocomputations tend to report only good news, while others' only bad.

The dimensions of architecture are the dimensions of perceptual space. The three spatial dimensions are, of course, and always have been, of high interest, but not always of the highest. A perfectly-proportioned Palladian room, for instance, can stimulate great admiration. But not if it happens to be on fire, or, less extremely, not, perhaps, if it is lit by a blinding beam of sunlight through a small window, or if it is painted pink and brown, or if the person standing in it has an aversion to Palladio. It is the three spatial dimensions that make the room, but it is those three plus all the others deemed relevant that make a *domain*.[1]

Herein, though, lies an ambiguity, and it is this: does a work of architecture describe a particular perceptual space all its own? Or is it something which exists in the perceptual spaces of the beholders, as it responds to many dimensions, which can go noticed or unnoticed, and which can, when noticed, be regarded positively or negatively? We think it is the latter.

The reasons we think so have to do with the nature of choice. In the former alternative, where architecture represents a perceptual space (presumably a replica of the architect's own, and of what he could and did care to measure), choices have been confronted. But they have also been made, and the only choice left to the beholder is to accept or refuse the whole set. In the latter alternative, choices have been recognized, but not actually made.

Lately there has been much talk among architects of "exclusive" and "inclusive" design (See pages 51-60). The one presumably seeks to purify itself and attain a powerful simplicity by severely limiting the range of images and forms it emulates. The other embraces a multitude of disparate references in its lurch toward catholicity. However, a more basic definition of "exclusivist" architecture may be the one contained in the alternatives just described above. For in the former case the observer is excluded from choice; in the latter he is not.

G.A.

Space

Space in architecture is a special category of free space, phenomenally created by the architect when he gives a part of free space shape and scale. Its first two dimensions — width and breadth — are responsive mainly to functional imperatives in the narrow sense, but the manipulation of its third dimension — height — grants the inhabitant's mind the special opportunity to develop yet other dimensions beyond.

Architects' words seem to rile people. We talk of "making" a space, and others point out that we have not made a space at all; it was there all along.[1] What we *have* done, or tried to do, when we cut a piece of space off from the continuum of all space, is to make it recognizable as a *domain*, responsive to the perceptual dimensions of its inhabitants.

Curiously, the acts the architect can most effectively perform with space appear to be opposing ones, though both seem to work. You can capture space or let it go, "define" it or "explode" it. Space is surely one of the few things that you have more of after you have "exploded" it, but it seems to thrive in captivity too. The failures come when we don't make it recognizable, when we do not distinguish a piece from the continuum.

It is easy to see why we fail so often. For one thing, we do not draw space, but rather plans and sections in which the space lurks. So there is a constant temptation to focus on objects rather than on the architectural space they breathe into existence. Drawing-board victories (like getting everything lined

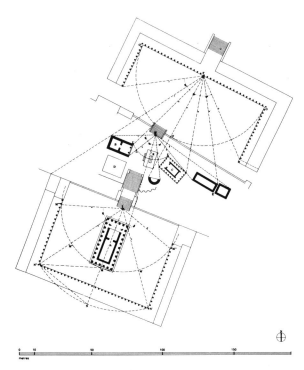

A Doric site: the Asclepeion, Cos, from C. A. Doxiadis' *Architectural Space in Ancient Greece* (1972)

up) replace and negate the real pleasures discoverable in space.

Architects' spatial enthusiasms have been heterogenous during the past decades. The principles of the Austrian planner Camillo Sitte[2] (rediscovered just after World War II and translated into English) were based on a fondness for medieval *piazze, plazas, places, and plätze*. Sitte stressed the importance of keeping their corners solid so the space could not escape. He was interested, too, in keeping the center of such spaces unencumbered by statues and other solid objects, so that the observer could stand there and feel that he was the center of a composition perceivable in its entirety. But the worst gaffe, as Sitte saw it, was to leave the corners open so that the space, no longer either contained or dramatically escaping, seemed to leak out and be lost.

Another great influence which has been present is an almost complete inversion of those rules. It lies behind the Baroque stage drawings of the Bibiena family and the architectural fantasies of Piranesi — especially his prisons, where ramps and stairs rise to mind-boggling distances in the almost limitless upper reaches of incomprehensible spaces. Yet another spatial construct has been found by Modern architects in the great mosque at Córdoba, where an orchard of columns fades into the dark distance and equivocates about the limits of the place and the position of spaces and objects in it.

Siegfried Giedion[3] sought to reconcile (or fudge) these contrasting spatial enthusiasms by postulating, in a sort of art-historical coda to Einstein's theory

8

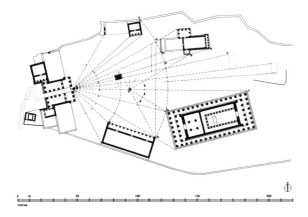

An Ionic site: the Acropolis III, Athens, from C. A. Doxiadis' *Architectural Space in Ancient Greece* (1972)

of relativity, the presumption that architectural space since the seventeenth century had become linked with time. But it is difficult indeed to square his thesis with the static and repetitive design of most Modern buildings.

A much more surprising (and in the end illuminating) thesis is the one set forward by the contemporary Greek planner C. A. Doxiadis.[4] It manages to jump clear of the Cartesian grid, which has so far contained most spatial arrangements, to discern in ancient Greek sites a radial organizing system. From the point of entry to a sacred area, 30-degree or 36-degree segments of a circle radiated. The corners of all buildings were then located on these radial lines, so that from the point of origin the buildings completely closed the view (in the Doric order) or opened a single segment to the surrounding landscape (in the Ionic order). Perhaps more important than the question of whether this was really the way the ancient Greeks did it, is the capacity of modern man to imagine such a system. It seems to be one of a number of signs that we, in our pluralism, are finally working clear of the rigid Cartesian grid, with its dictatorship of the right angle, by which Modern architecture has so firmly been gripped. It represents a sign that space is beginning to be understood from the point of view of the person perceiving or experiencing it — not as a mathematical abstraction.

Another sign, reinforced by psychoanalytic literature, is the return of body-centered space. Psychiatrists have noted that as children we first perceive that

9

up is different from down, and left from right, and that front is very different from back. But as we grow up we are gradually disabused of the notion that the three spatial dimensions do have *moral* significance. Now, however, these archaic truths are once again beginning to be taken as the basis for organizing the space we pluck out of the continuum.

Again, space in architecture — whatever its organizing impulse — is of interest to us in only two ways: either because of its orderly containment or because of the drama of its escape. The pleasures of a serene and carefully proportioned contained space (like a Palladian double-cube room) can for us coexist with the excitement of a twentieth-century spatial explosion (like the U. S. Pavilion at Expo '67 or the Matterhorn at Disneyland).

C.M.

Shape

Shape calls attention to things and their meanings. Architects, whether they mean to or not, give shape to things, and the people who see or inhabit those things, whether in full consciousness or not, respond to these shapes. The dimensions of this response are somewhat difficult to measure, since they consist of personal as well as more general components. Architects from the beginning have tried to compile systems and formulate rules of proportion and composition which would aid them in evoking responses from the people who saw the shapes they made.

The notion of grown people shaping things has been seen by many during the past half century as an act somewhere between the unfashionable and the illicit. Function, it was supposed, would give form a run for its money, and the less attention paid to shape the better. In the 1940s, for instance, a favorite drawing was of an absurd airplane, presumably designed by an architect. It was unable to fly under its deadweight of misunderstood talismen, columns, pediments, and walls of crumbling stone.

By the 1960s the arrogance of architects imposing a shape on things was under attack on social grounds, and form-givers (which means people who shape things) were labelled as cultural dinosaurs. The presumption was either that good things shouldn't have any shape (in the same way a good society would not need any government) or that the shape of the environment would come, without midwifery, out of the interaction of users and makers. These

11

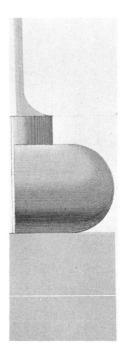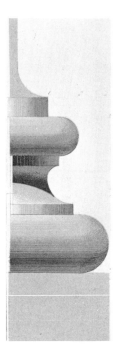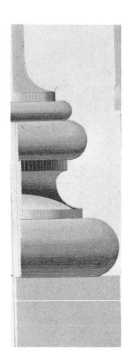

Bases of the five orders of columns, by Samual Sloan, from *Sloan's Constructive Architecture* (1859)

presumptions, of course, were wrong. They foundered because function, by itself, is inadequate to define a single shape for a building. Since any functional problem can be solved by many different shapes, the choice is bound to depend on the preferences of the makers.

So we are still faced with the need to give things shape, and architects should note the nature of the guidelines there are.

One distinction provides help — that between shape and form. Form, as we have been told, follows function. It delimits an arena in which things can take — that is, be given — shape. Spoons, for instance, are normally devices with a concave surface for holding liquids, with a handle attached to facilitate movement of the liquid and to provide protection for human hands in case the liquid is hot. There are billions of possible shapes a spoon can take, though there is only one form. The choice of shapes will be based on various cultural and personal standards. Or there is the interesting possibility that, for the task at hand, a spoon is not needed at all, and that a bowl or a siphon or a pump or a pipe will do the job better. Or there are cases in which the requirements of the form of the spoon have been violated, so that all the liquid leaks out, and no connections in the mind and memory, however poignant, can overcome the formal failure.

Of shape itself there are three measures: those that we all share (archetypal), those we share with a culture (cultural), and those that are a product of our own memories (personal).

12

Archetypal shapes depend on an ancient dialectic between columns and walls. Since humankind came out of the caves, we have erected columns and spread out walls, and from an orchestration of those two acts we have developed the art of building. Our columns have consistently enough been taken as male fertility symbols, but they have an even more enduring role as celebrations of the upright stance of humans. Our walls surely recall the cave, and the womb of the earth, but they exalt as well, by the ways in which they are arranged, the skill of the geometrician and the occasional triumph of reason. The plans of buildings and of cities to this day are traces of columns and walls, and in civilizations from Philadelphia to Japan they still provide the basis for design.

Attempts to reach eternal harmonies through the proper relations of dimensions come close to being archetypal; at any rate they bridge many cultures. Andrea Palladio[1] was interested in the relation of whole numbers, designing rooms so that the relation of the length to the width would be the same as the relation of width to height. The prevalence of the Golden Mean in the natural world and in the preferences of human beings has often been noted. The Golden Mean probably shows up most clearly in the Fibonacci series of numbers, where on a base of one and one, each succeeding number is the sum of the two previous numbers: 1, 1, 2, 3, 5, 8, 13, 21, 34, 55, etc. This relation, drawn as a series of squares, forms the basis for a spiral. The same spiral can be found in a snail's shell, and it traces the creature's growth. The same configuration was

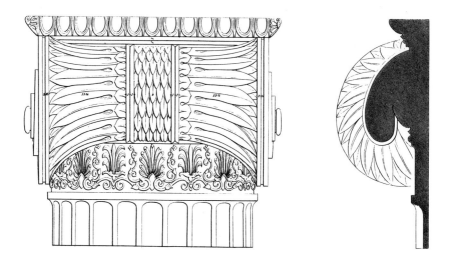

Ionic capitals, by Asher Benjamin, from *The Architect* (1845)

also long ago appropriated for the volutes of the capital of an Ionic column. Even now, people, when tested, seem to show a strong preference for rectangles in the proportion of any two succeeding numbers in the Fibonacci series past the first two. The possibility of growth, one takes it, is discernible in the shape, and that presumably explains its appeal.

Some preferences for shape are cultural. Gothic builders were excited by verticality. It is hardly surprising, therefore, that the preference which was developed in their soaring cathedrals extended also to pointed windows on houses and pointed tops on boxes and chairbacks. No surprise, either, that it was taken over whole by nineteenth century romantics, who were able to read moral rectitude and spiritual enlightenment into the verticality of pointed architecture, and only worldliness into more horizontal shapes. Esthetic tilts between Gothic and Classical styles grew astonishingly vicious. But if we start to feel at all superior because of our distance from these horrid little wars of taste, we need only note the fervor with which contemporary clients state their preferences for materials; the choice of natural wood or white walls has become a kind of Rubicon of architectural decision.

Cultural preferences for one shape over another slope quite quickly into personal preferences, based partly on what we have been taught, but mostly on our memories. The sound of an outboard motor across a lake may be for some people less likely to stir up concerns about the energy crisis than to recall a

carefree childhood summer. And several patterns of mullions which may divide the same window opening might have connotations — dimensions — very different from each other, depending on the connotations they have in our own experience, the places loved or scorned out of our own pasts.

So, in the end, what is the architect to do in the face of the endless diversity of human experience, the presence of personal as well as cultural and archetypal components to our perceptions of shapes? One useful part of the response is to render unto the mind's eye what is the mind's eye's, but to take care that the images do not interfere with flexibility of human use — to keep, as it were, the myth up off the floor.[2] Also, it seems to us useful to regard design as the choreography of the familiar and the unfamiliar — the chance to massage our sensibilities with shapes that are likely to be familiar to us (whatever their specific connotation to our individual lives) and shapes or relationships full of surprise, which call us to attention and response, readying us for choice.

C.M.

Classic doorway, by Samual Sloan, from *Sloan's Constructive Architecture* (1859)

Scale

As shape has to do with the meaning of individual things, scale has to do with their physical size, and therefore their importance and their meaning in relation to something else. No matter how unimportant or plain it may be, every part of every building has a size. And so scale, which involves arranging various sizes in some order, and choosing particular sizes when the option is available, is of great interest to all architects, and it is very much talked about.

But often it is nevertheless not entirely clear just what scale really is. We talk, for instance, of a large-scale housing development, and we usually mean just that it is big. In a different context, we say that an architectural drawing has a scale, meaning that so many units of measure on the drawing represent so many units of measure in the actual building. Then there are super scale, miniature scale, monumental scale, and — perhaps the most talked about of all — human scale.

People use all these terms presumably because they mean something. So the problem in talking about scale is not to exclude any of these possible meanings, but instead to find some common intent in them all. One common intent is this: whenever the word scale is used, something is being compared with something else. The large-scale housing development is large in comparison to an average housing development. The scale of the architectural drawing notes the size of the rendered building in comparison to the real thing. Super scale usually means that something is much bigger than we might have ex-

17

pected, miniature scale that it is much smaller. Monumental scale presumably means that something is the size of a monument (whatever that may be), and human scale must mean that something is the size of a person (whatever *that* may be).

The objects singled out for comparison are all different — a drawing, a building complex, a single building, or just a part. Different also are the things the objects are being compared to — another building complex, a single building, our expectations, the presumed size of a monument, and our own presumed size. What is consistent is that the size of something is always being compared to the size of something else and a conclusion drawn from that. Thus scale is not the same thing as size; scale is *relative* size, the size of something relative to something else.

Relative to what else? There are many possibilities, which is precisely why the manipulation of scale is so useful a tool in architecture. Among the alternatives are these:

Relative to the whole. Since buildings are made up of parts, the size of the parts relative to the whole can constitute a scale. The facade of a typical Georgian house, for instance, will have windows in it. No matter how big the facade or how big the windows, they will have a scale that results from the relationship of the one to the other.

Relative to other parts. If one window in the same facade is larger or smaller

18

A four-story street front, by M. F. Cummings and C. C. Miller, from *Architecture* (1865)

than the others, no matter what the actual size of either, another scale results, and often this can be a signal that something particularly important is going on behind the differently-sized window.

Relative to usual size. Most kinds of things have, within certain rough limits, a usual size. Double-hung windows do, and so, for instance, do fireplaces, and bricks, and standard pieces of wood, and plaster moldings. If any of these are very much bigger or smaller than usual, they have bigger or smaller scale on the basis of that relationship alone. This is one of the reasons why supergraphics seemed interesting to many people in the 1960s, because they were much bigger than graphics usually were. It is also why they no longer seem very interesting very often; they are no longer very unusual.

Relative to human size. Certain things that people use directly have certain approximate sizes. For purposes of human use these sizes may be constrained by minimum and maximum limits, like a door knob, or by only a minimum one, like a door. Door knobs, doors — and with them seats, counters, beds, stairs, and all the rest — have necessarily a "human" scale. Their sizes are related to the dimensions of the human body; otherwise people can't use them. Curiously, though, it is only in relation to these kinds of things that the term "human scale" seems to have a precise meaning.

The problems in a more general use of the term begin, of course, with the obvious fact that, since people vary in size, it would be hard to dimension all the parts of a building to the size of the human body precisely — though Le Corbusier, for instance, with his proportional system *Le Modulor,* and Frank Lloyd Wright, with a series of Procrustean beds, have tried (see page 55). In fact, though, this kind of dimensioning is not very often attempted.

Second, it is quite hard for a person to perceive the size of something relative to his or her size unless that something is fairly close to that size. Thus it is easy to tell that a six-foot six-inch ceiling is near to human size, whereas it is not so easy to recognize that an eleven-foot six-inch ceiling is about twice human size. What is likely to have more immediate impact is the recognition that such a ceiling is usual for certain kinds of rooms, and that recognition may provide either an ironic or expected enforcement to the sense one has of the particular room one is in. Similarly, if you walk through a thirty-foot door, you are much less likely to remark that it is more than five times your height as you are to notice that it is very big *for a door.*

Finally, it is also quite hard for a person to perceive the size of something relative to his or her size unless that something is fairly nearby. Otherwise the idea of usual scale is, again, much more likely to come into play. The size of a building in the distance, for example, is understandable mainly in terms of how big that kind of building and its identifiable parts are likely to be — though even that, as we shall see, can be a source of surprise.

The term "human scale" does, nevertheless, have a broader meaning, and

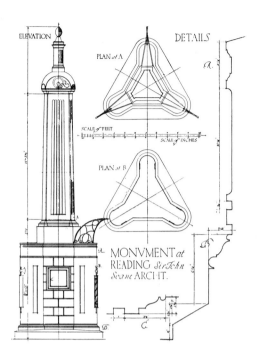

ELEVATION

DETAILS

PLAN at A

PLAN at B

SCALE 9 FEET
SCALE 9 INCHES

A. MONVMENT at
READING Sir John
Soane ARCHT.

Monument by Sir John Soane, from M. E. Macartney's *Practical Exemplar of Architecture* (1909)

we clearly intend something when we use it. It seems, ironically, that this meaning lies more in the realm of shape than of scale, and in particular that it lies in the realm of shapes that have human meaning. A window in a wall, no matter what its size, can be most memorable for the implication that there may be someone behind it to look out. It is like other windows we know where this has happened, or where we ourselves have looked out. This is a function of shape, not scale. In general, the building which uses shapes that bear human meaning is more likely to feel human than the building that merely tries to replicate the dimensions of the body. The former is what we mean by "human scale."

It is interesting to note, too, that the other difficult term "monumental scale," also has its meaning more in the realm of shape than of scale. Monuments can, after all, be very tiny indeed, and what seems to signal "monument" may be a stark and simple shape (like an obelisk) or one with an even more specific cultural connotation (like a Latin cross).

One of the powers of architectural scale is that it is not confined to one set of relationships. Scale is an elaborate and complex coding system whereby things, by their sizes, can at one fell swoop be related to some whole, to each other, to other things like them, and to people. The result of all these computations can be a calm and clear message in which an ordered hierarchy of things is revealed with no surprises on any count. The message can also contain some

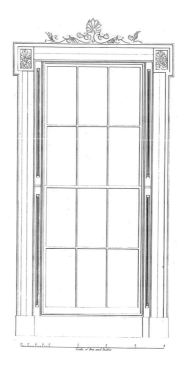
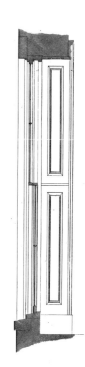

Double hung window, by Asher Benjamin, from *The Architect* (1845)

obvious distortions. Most interesting, perhaps, is when the message seems a choreography of both, offering a clearly perceptible order on some terms, and a set of surprises and ambiguities on some others. Then scale works in the service of the inclusivist attitude which, rather than presenting the observer with answers ("This is what it is"), includes the observer by urging him or her to ask a question, ("What is this?"). Scale can then be a device which helps achieve a quality that all good buildings possess: being at once "like" something (and having a general meaning) while also being special (and having a particular meaning).

St. Peter's in Rome is almost always mentioned in discussions of scale, and it is usually called an example of a "trick" of scale. In fact, the reason why the manipulation of scale at St. Peter's is so memorable is precisely that in some respects there is no trick at all. The relationship of each of the parts (windows, doors, columns and all the rest) to each other and to the whole seems altogether normal on the basis of our experience of similar buildings. What is not normal, of course, is that the size of each of these things in relation to their usual size — and, we discover when we get close, their relationship to us — is wildly large. Here two kinds of scale are colliding with two other kinds, and the effect depends as much on the normality of the one pair as on the eccentricity of the other. The collision is made clear during the time it takes us to approach the building.

Doric column by Owen Biddle, from *The Young Carpenter's Assistant* (1805).

Multiple scales can also be revealed all at once. One of the obvious places this can happen is on the facade of a building where two sets of similar elements are rendered at different sizes, and therefore in different relationships to the whole. The question then arises as to what the dominant system is, and what indeed is the whole that is made up of apparently disparate parts.

Scale, of course, can be — and most often is — combined with shape, thereby increasing still further the number of possible variations available to the architect. A Doric column is different from a double-hung window not only because it is usually bigger but also because it has a different shape. Thus a building with sets of both things has a double scale, because each set has a different size in relation to the whole.

Similar manipulations of scale alone, or of scale in combination with shape, occur inside rooms. Sometimes the variation in size is between things with the same shapes — not only windows and doors, but furniture and moldings and floor boards — and sometimes it is between things of different shapes. For example, all of the parts — furniture, doors, windows, walls, floors, and ceilings — can be sized in a usual way, thus having a normal and orderly relationship to each other and to the whole. But then the hierarchical chain can be interrupted by some additional thing — a fireplace, for instance — that is dramatically bigger or smaller than one would expect. What is the whole of which this different element is a part? Which whole is more vivid — the one we can see, supported by the scale of everything else in the room? Or the one we can't see, suggested by the surprising size of the dissonant object?

The ways in which different kinds of scales can be combined are legion. Again, these combinations can be bought by the architect for free, since every part of a building has to have a size, and that size will automatically have some relationship to the whole thing, to the other parts, to the usual size of that particular part, and to people. The question naturally arises as to which of these relationships are worth emphasis. Earlier, we noted a similar predicament with dimensions. We proposed a solution in the form of a question, "What do you care to measure?" The solution to the problem of how the relative size of things (their scale) is treated is, in kind, identical: "What relationships do you care to call attention to?"

G.A.

St. Thomas Church: Serving two spaces

One of the oldest traditions in architecture is tradition itself — the use of understood and proven precedents which are partly repeated, partly modified to make a new building. No matter what architects say, they all rely on tradition. It may be an old one (Georgian) or it may be fairly new (Modern), and it may even be the latest fad brought from the drafting room of a fashionable architecture school. But tradition will not be ignored, because a knowledge of what might be done under a particular set of circumstances — and how, in fact, it has been done — is too useful a tool of architectural practice, just as it is one of the cornerstones of architectural education. Such knowledge guides the architect through a bewildering variety of specific choices, emphasizing certain possibilities while giving others lower priority. Glass walls and exposed steel enclosing a rectilinear space, for instance, carry with them a host of suggestions for making the rest of the building, just as do walls of rough wood or shingles around a plan shot through with surprising diagonals. Traditions also conjure up images for both the inhabitant and the architect; they provide a set of alternatives for what a building might actually look like as well as how it can be formed. And a knowledge of what has been done in the past obviously avoids the useless reinvention of the wheel (happily leaving more time for those wheels that really do need reinventing).

Ralph Adams Cram and Bertram Goodhue, the designers of the 1911 St. Thomas Church in New York City, paid notable attention to architectural

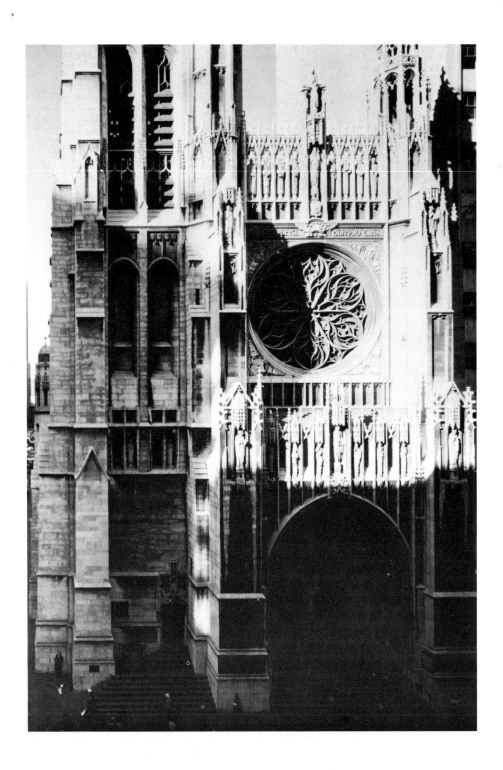

tradition, and in fact they did so with so much erudition and scholarship that most of us now are likely to think of them as merely — to use that faintly derogatory word — "traditional" architects. St. Thomas Church certainly *looks* traditional, and people who remember it remember it most often for the abundance and elegance of its Gothic detail. Cram and Goodhue clearly understood the power that well-known architectural images have over the mind, and they knew just which set seemed appropriate in this case, and how to make them correctly. They also knew how traditional forms could be used to solve traditional problems like walling in an interior space and covering it over and lighting it.

It may therefore seem surprising that the building which resulted is, in many ways, boldly original, having finally about as much to do with real Gothic architecture as the town of Chartres has to do with Manhattan. For Cram and Goodhue seem to have used traditional precedents in a particularly selective way — not just to provide formal models for each of the parts and a controlling image for the whole, but as a measure of what was usual and what was unique about the design problem at hand. That is, if a tradition — any tradition — is taken as the framework for a particular design, then part of it will fit and part of it most probably will not, and will have to be modified. If, as in the case of St. Thomas Church, the chosen tradition has extensive associations, then the ways it fits and the ways it doesn't each take on an unusual

28

importance. Thus St. Thomas Church — indeed, like any worthy piece of architecture — speaks as vividly of the particular (this church in a modern city) as of the general (the Church). It is this combination of particular and general, original and traditional — and not some literal brand of architectural historicizing — that makes the building worth revisiting in the late twentieth century.

Ralph Adams Cram and Bertram Goodhue were partners in the firm of Cram, Goodhue and Ferguson of New York and Boston, and together they designed a number of important buildings in the early twentieth century — most of them Gothic in style and religious in program (including the chapel of the United States Military Academy at West Point). Cram, like many other Gothic Revivalists in England and America, was grandiosely spiritual in his allegiance to the style, attaching to it a very moral significance. So great was his fervor that he insisted, for instance, on building St. Thomas Church, except for the roof truss,[1] entirely out of masonry in the traditional manner, without the aid of structural steel. "False construction," he wrote, "is simply a lie told for reasons of penury or ostentation."[2] Unfortunately, though, due to a miscalculation, steel had to be added later to keep the north wall from collapsing.[3]

Goodhue seems to have been a little more easygoing in his approach, regarding Gothic as only one alternative among many, rather than the One True Way. When the firm of Cram, Goodhue and Ferguson was dissolved in 1914, just as the major part of St. Thomas Church was being finished, he went on to

design buildings in various other styles, including the exuberantly "Spanish" theme building for the Panama-Pacific Exhibition in San Diego and the starkly pre-Modern Nebraska State Capitol at Lincoln. Because Goodhue became one of the most original of the established architects practicing in America in the early twentieth century, and because part of the originality of St. Thomas Church consists of the boxy, chunky massing so characteristic of Goodhue's work, it is hard to resist thinking that he had the upper hand in the building's design. Indeed, with the recent wave of general interest in American buildings before the *blitzkrieg* of Modern architecture, enthusiasts have attributed St. Thomas Church to Goodhue — partly, one supposes, because it so clearly reflects talent, something which Goodhue clearly had, in contrast to his partner Cram, who from this perspective seems a little pedantic and pompous. However, scholars and partisans of Cram are adamant in insisting that the building is mainly by him, and they have some evidence to prove their point.[4]

In any case, the design problem was this: how to provide seating for a large number of people (as well as space for offices and other parochial activities) on a relatively small urban site, and how to make a building that, from the outside, could remain a firm presence in the city as its surroundings changed, as they inevitably must.

The solution to the first part of the problem is as straightforward as it is unorthodox. The main interior space of the building extends from virtually

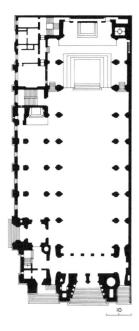

Plan of St. Thomas Church (above left)
The interior of St. Thomas Church in 1914, before the installation of the reredos (above right)
The nave, choir, and reredos of St. Thomas Church (opposite)

the front of the site to the very back, and it is wrenched off center to the north, leaving just enough room for offices and a side chapel with a gallery above on the south (53rd Street) side. The most remarkable feature of the interior, which is otherwise dignified in a solid and rather plain way, is the enormous reredos above the altar at the (geographical) west end; it was designed by Goodhue and Lee Lawrie, a versatile artist who was later responsible for some of the best sculpture in Rockefeller Center (page viii), and its ivory-colored stone contrasts with the warmer and darker sandstone of the rest of the interior. Though all of the figures in it conform to a carefully planned iconography, the reredos as a whole reads most strongly as a rich and delicate texture. In architectural terms the most instructive thing about it is that it is an object lesson in making virtue of necessity, for the sense of depth and lightness created by the multitude of niches and canopies in the reredos betrays the fact that, with the exception of three small windows high above the floor, this end of the building is actually a blank wall that abuts the adjacent parish house and, beyond that, the Museum of Modern Art.

Similarly, the north wall of the building is blank, though that fact is obscured by the much more dominant clerestory windows which are set some ten feet back from the lot line and are identical to those on the south side of the nave. Thus there is a great deal of *seeming* here (architectural dishonesty, some would say), and partial likenesses are everywhere being created. The result is that

The chapel on the south side of the nave (above)
The north wall of the nave of St. Thomas Church (opposite)

what is in fact a space set off center in an asymmetrical plan and walled in on two sides by adjacent buildings is made to feel central and unencumbered — and Gothic to boot.

The asymmetrical plan which is a peculiar feature of the interior also plays an important part in solving the second part of the design problem — making a building that can hold its own in the changing urban scene. When seen in elevation, the facade of St. Thomas Church seems truncated and almost bizarre — two thirds of a Gothic facade, consisting of a massive and rather stubby tower and a more delicately ornamented "central" portal and rose window. The building, of course, has almost never been seen this way except by a draftsman, or by an adventurous architectural photographer, and the knowledge that it would not must certainly have been one of the justifications for designing it like this. Normally, when the facade is seen straight on, the observer is at street level and fairly close by; from this perspective the projecting portal with its deep-set doors and wide stairs dominates, obscuring the eccentricity of the rest. When the building is seen from any distance at all, it must be from some point up or down the avenue, and from such an angle the tower — which is designed for solidity rather than for graceful height, in what would be futile competition with its neighbors — becomes by far the most dominant element.

Why, nevertheless, does it make any sense at all to organize a building in this way, except for the fact that such an organization reflects to some extent

St·Thomas·Church·New·York·City

CRAM GOODHUE AND FERGVSON ARCHITECTS NEW YORK & BOSTON

The main entrance to St. Thomas Church, seen from across Fifth Avenue (above left)
St. Thomas Church from Fifth Avenue (above right)
Architects' rendering of a preliminary design for St. Thomas Church (opposite)

the arrangement of the spaces inside? The answer to this question, insofar as it suggests a general attitude, has very important implications, which architects can choose to ignore only at their peril (and the peril of those who have to live with their buildings). Unlike many other buildings, St. Thomas Church is not composed around itself, nor indeed is it composed with any detailed regard for its immediate neighbors (all of which, incidentally, have changed since the building was built). Instead, the exterior of the church allies itself with what is perhaps the most basic, and almost certainly the most permanent, feature of its surroundings — the city block and the city street. The outsize proportions of the square tower make it seem to the eye to mark the corner of Fifth Avenue and 53rd Street as surely as it marks the corner of the building, and the rest of the facade, not stopped by a second tower on the north, makes a gesture of continuity with its neighbors on this side of the block.

Regarding this gesture, it is interesting to note that in the late 1950s the architects and owners of Canada House (now called the Mutual Benefit Life Building) paid careful attention to St. Thomas Church when they designed and built their new building immediately to the north on Fifth Avenue by echoing the church's color, and by silhouetting it against a plain and windowless south wall. Such urban courtesy is certainly not to be discounted, since it is rather rare. But one can't help wondering whether or not, in this special case where the older building is so strong, it was so meticulously required — whether

A part of the north wall of St. Thomas Church, seen from the Fifth Avenue sidewalk (above)
St. Thomas Church just after the construction of Canada House in the late 1950s (opposite)

it would not have been enough simply to respect the format of street and sidewalk and facade (as St. Thomas Church does), rather than to set the main mass of the new building back behind a small plaza (which is what happened with Canada House). In any case, the setback results in the anomaly of exposing a part of the church's north wall, which was clearly designed to abut an adjacent building.

Perhaps with all their good will the architects of Canada House mistook the older building for an elegant and fragile curiosity to be treated with delicate respect, rather than the fundamentally urban piece of architecture it is, able to hold its own among its neighbors as long as they respected the same rules. This would be a mistake easy to make, but worth correcting, because St. Thomas Church, in its close allegiance to the structure of the city and in its manifest concern for the way a building is perceived by people (rather than for some abstract formal construct in the architect's mind), tells of a kind of architecture that is radically different from much that we have become accustomed to.

It is different because as a whole thing (or, for that matter, as a collection of parts) the building does not make that kind of coherent, self-contained sense that architects often strive for in their designs. The plan makes sense mainly in terms of the central interior space, *as perceived from the inside.* The facade makes sense mainly *as perceived from the street.* The late architect Louis I. Kahn made the celebrated distinction between architectural space that is "served"

39

and space that is "servant" — the former subject to the most disciplined dimensioning that the architect (and the perceiver) could marshall, and the other formed requisitely to complete the interstices. With St. Thomas Church, the "served" spaces are two: the church interior and the street; the "building" is servant to them both. What we remember, remarkably, is them as much as it.

G.A.

Action Architecture: The Santa Barbara County Courthouse and Le Corbusier's Carpenter Center

St. Thomas Church is an exciting building because it so vividly captures the powerful images of Gothic architecture without really being like any other Gothic building in the world, and because it is composed in a way that lets it reinforce and confirm the urban landscape in which it stands. At the other edge of the North American continent and in a completely different landscape, another building — the Santa Barbara County Courthouse, designed by William Mooser and completed in 1929 — exhibits a remarkably similar set of architectural urges, and the results are at least as moving.

Santa Barbara[1] lies on a narrow plain between the steep Santa Ynez Mountains and the Pacific Ocean. Here the climate is wondrously benign, and the place is filled with the exoticism of California. This is an exoticism that consists (or used to consist, in the days when the courthouse was conceived) of an incredible landscape and of delicate, languorous, and very far away images of Spain, whose colonizers had anciently strung out their 21 missions across what is now the state. The half-forgotten, shadowy remnants of Spanish architecture seemed, in the 1920s, to capture the mood of Santa Barbara, and people set out to bolster it and extend it, creating an Anglo-Californian vision of Spanish romance. In 1925, the Scottish architect James Osborne Craig completed El Paseo, a labyrinth of courtyards, passages, and open rooms that house many small shops and a splendid, balconied restaurant open to the sky. One of its parts, the "Street in Spain," bounded by glowing white stucco walls and

41

The "Street in Spain" in El Paseo, by James Osborne Craig (above)
The Santa Barbara County Courthouse, by William Mooser (opposite)

colorful awnings, slips between two historic abodes built in the early nineteenth century, which become a part of the newly-created ensemble.

Craig's work here — plus the work of the distinguished Santa Barbara architect George Washington Smith — turned people on to the excitement of "Spanish" architecture. It established an architectural idiom of white stucco walls, big-leafed plants, bougainvillea, low-pitched Mediterranean tile roofs, and gentle silhouettes against the deep blue sky. When Santa Barbara suffered a disastrous earthquake in 1925 and was faced with the task of rebuilding itself, this idiom was dramatically extended, resulting in a really remarkable case of the intentional assumption of an architectural style by a whole town (pages 111-112).

William Mooser's courthouse, the consummate gesture for all this enthusiasm, is at once a catalogue and a synthesis of all the things that the Santa Barbarans and their architects were up to. It is a confection that is like many things, but accurate to nothing. There is no precise, scholarly adherence to anything, but, in establishing its own principles, the building pays passionate, romantic allegiance to a half-imagined past.

What is most exciting about it is not just its windows and doors and details (each of them like something), but the whole thing, which is like only itself. As with St. Thomas Church, the courthouse is not just a building composed around itself and sitting in isolation on its site. Instead, it is a fragment of

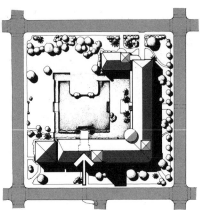

Plan of the Santa Barbara County Courthouse (above right)
Entrance to the Hall of Records (above left)

scenery that is composed to, and scaled to, the giant landscape — in this case, not an urban landscape, but a plain between the mountains and the sea.

Through the most daring manipulations of scale, individual pieces of the building swell to the most surprising proportions, far beyond the size required merely for human use, and certainly beyond our expectations — but just the right size for the making of a central public place in this setting. A great Gothic arch on one side of the building, for instance, breaks back through a series of smaller and smaller Gothic arches to what becomes, suddenly and without transition, a small entrance way, almost half of which is blocked by a white wall with a tiny cottage window in it. The other half has a door and two even tinier windows, so that the huge opening has suddenly turned back into a domestic-size entrance; you go in the little door and find yourself in the Hall of Records.

Vignettes like this are held together in the building by the huge white walls with giant plants casting their shadows upon them. The building pretends to be Spanish, but the pretension has a particular kind of connection with nature that is nothing like Spain, whose builders never had the chance to make an unfortified assemblage like this, and indeed whose traditions of place-making tended in the opposite direction, turning away from the vaster landscape into enclosed plazas and couryards.[2]

The main entrance to the Santa Barbara County Courthouse is a truly monumental arch that leads not into the building but straight through it —

44

Main entrance to the Santa Barbara County Courthouse

straight into a view of the mountain range. The arch is a Propylaea to the entire landscape, and the Spanish epigraph above it — translated above the smaller doorway on the right, which actually leads inside — documents the juxtaposition that is being made: "God gave us the fields; the skill of man built cities."

In itself, this arch is an extraordinary composition of high originality, a curious choreography of familiar and unfamiliar images. It is framed by a cornice and by two vaguely Corinthian columns that do not even begin until almost half way up. The column on the right comes down to its base the way a column normally should, but the other one seems locked in various blocks of not-quite-quarried stone. These blocks randomly cascade down into a pool, which is coped with a fat molding that looks like the base of some other column, and from the pool rise a pair of naturalistic sculptures of the period.

All of this is not like anything in particular. But — in terms of shape and scale, at least — it is all very monumental. Thus it comes as a jolt to notice that other pieces of the composition are not monumental at all, but instead are downright domestic — like the hacienda-style tile roof with its big overhang, or the little cottage window with shutters, or the larger grilled window that might have been lifted from the facade of some house in Seville.

It comes as a surprise, too, to note the almost reckless abandon with which all the different pieces are assembled, and the stupefyingly kinetic feeling that

Main entrance (above left)
Main entrance and tower (above right)
The courtyard of the Santa Barbara County Courthouse (opposite top)
A performance in the courtyard during the Santa Barbara Fiesta (opposite bottom)

the whole building acquires. The center of the big arch, for instance, misses its alignment with the peak of the roof above, which is being pulled by the arch in one direction and the tower in the other, lodging itself somewhere in between. The arches in the white stucco wall to the right of the big arch are really enormous, almost tearing away the building as they march toward the entrance. Everywhere there are extreme contrasts. Notice how big the scale of the clock face is, and how incredibly tiny the little square window under the peak of the eaves. Or note how thick and plastic the stucco walls and the timber brackets are, and how thin and spindly the iron brackets that support the tower balcony. The building is responding to no calm voice telling it to sit there and be still. Everything is being yanked and pulled and squeezed and swung around by everything else that is here — including the giant landscape.

The courtyard, enclosed on just a little over two sides, is a garden, and it contains a partial stage for the newly-made rituals of the annual fiesta that was devised in the 1920s, and which continues today. When you enter through the main arch and are faced with the view of the mountains in the distance, the garden obligingly drops down seven or eight steps to get itself out of the way. Behind you is the back of the main arch, extended in rough stone across the stucco in a kind of up-and-down stairstep that is quite different from anything else that is happening nearby. Most of the rest of the openings in the courtyard walls are simple, but, again, they come in a considerable array of shapes and

The Santa Barbara County Jail, overlooking the courtyard (above left)
Detail of the Carpenter Center (above right)

sizes, and they are composed in a syncopated and polyphonic way, dancing across the surfaces of the white walls.

One of the most spirited dances occurs opposite the main entrance to the courtyard on one of the damnedest walls ever devised, which is the wall of the Santa Barbara County Jail. It looks like some kind of coded message of round, rounded, rectangular, and square openings, like holes arcanely punched in a computer card so that the spacings as well as the shapes mean something. Almost nothing lines up vertically with anything else, but everything seems to bear some careful relationship to everything else in a complicated development of big and little, vertical and horizontal. It is like the Chicago jazz of the 1920s — a set of notes, not extraordinary in themselves, being blown to a formula of syncopated rhythms that make it all amazing. If we knew how to read the windows, we could sing their song.

One of the many impressive things about Le Corbusier's famous Carpenter Center for the Visual Arts at Harvard University is how very close in spirit it is to the Santa Barbara County Courthouse. It has, like the courthouse, a collection of valued images, but here the images are those of America which Le Corbusier (who had never before built on this continent, except for his contribution to the United Nations) thought of as being the spirit of the modern United States. The idiom is Tennessee Valley Authority concrete — except that it is thin, since this is a building and not a dam. The way the concrete is used

48

Detail of the Carpenter Center (above left)
The Carpenter Center, Harvard University, Cambridge, Massachusetts, by Le Corbusier (above right)

embodies a careful set of recalls that are as redolent as possible of the idiom of the exciting new American way. Le Corbusier never used concrete anywhere else in quite this light and spacy way, and the thick-and-thin play of the metal rails and glass blocks against it makes the whole seem more industrial, less lithic, than most of his other later work.

Through the middle of the Carpenter Center, with all its concrete and glass block and other pieces of American things, rolls an enormous pedestrian ramp. It is a raised version of the big arch at the Santa Barbara County Court-house, for it connects the building to its smaller and more urban landscape. Other things connect it too, like the stairs shown above, which look like something that might go up the side of a public works building, and which leap out to gulp in the adjacent space.

Set diagonally to the Fogg Museum on one side and the Faculty Club on the other, the building catches them both up in a dance. Instead of using windows, Le Corbusier uses surfaces of glass — knowing (as most contemporary architects do not seem to) that when the glass is in the light it will be reflective and when it is set back in the shadows it will be transparent, so that you can see what is going on inside. So as you are walking by, the glass on the outer surface reflects buildings across the street, and, since the building is at an angle to the neighbors, it catches them up dizzily. You are aware of them as well as it, and, in not an unfriendly way, it sets them on their ear.

49

The Carpenter Center

At the Carpenter Center and at the Santa Barbara County Courthouse there are collections of images that people found exciting, and hoped other people would find exciting too. In each case, the images are by definition like something. But the ways in which they are put together create buildings that are unlike anything that has happened before or since. The power that visual images like these have is something the human mind is always responsive to and has forever cared about. The business of being "correct" is of dramatically less interest. What is of special interest, and excitement, is the way these buildings take as active and free-wheeling a posture towards their settings as they do to their imaginistic forebearers, becoming catalysts that bring alive whole landscapes.

G.A. & C.M.

Inclusive and Exclusive[1]

If architects are to continue to do useful work on this planet, then surely their proper concern must be the creation of *place* — the ordered imposition of man's self on specific locations across the face of the earth. To make a place is to make a domain that helps people know where they are and, by extension, know who they are.

The most powerful places which our forebears made for themselves, and left for us, exist as a series of contiguous spaces. They organize a hierarchy of importance — first dividing what is inside from what is outside, then somehow arranging the inside things in some order. Objects confer importance to location, and location confers importance on objects. In Peking an axis penetrates from the outside of the city through layer after layer of walls to the seat of the emperor himself. In Hindu towns caste determines location from clean to dirty along the stream which serves everyone. The visible hierarchical order of these places was buttressed by the shared confidence that it was expressive of the order of the world, or indeed of the universe. The temple of Angkor Wat, with its cross axes and its concentric rings of temples, provides a diagram of heaven which recalls the concentric rings of mountains around the seven seas which center on the sacred Buddhist mountain.

Our own perceptions, however, like our own lives, are not bound to one particular place. Our order is not made of single inside, neatly separated from another outside, in which we can structure a visible simulation of our world.

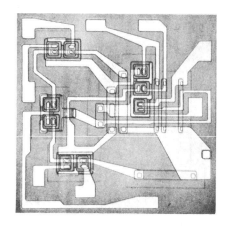

A printed circuit

The world that means the most to us (as everyone from Buckminster Fuller to Marshall McLuhan has pointed out) is no longer very visible anyway.

Many of us have stamping grounds which exist in separate places ending at one airport and picking up again at some other one. No matter where our bodies are at any moment, we can have "instant anywhere" by making immediate electronic contact with people anywhere on the face of the globe. We can even revel in the vicarious pleasure of blasting people off the face of the earth in order to be able to make contact with them in outer space.

This is to say that our new places are given form with electronic, rather than visual, glue. This electronic glue, of course, has some limitations. It can be argued, for instance, that although a great deal of preliminary maneuvering in courtship can occur over the telephone, face-to-face contact is still required for any real consummation of the activity.

About the time that architects and planners started to bleat about human scale (as if it had to do entirely with man's body and not at all with his mind or his ideas) and to rhapsodize about the pleasures of sitting in the *Piazza di San Marco* (the heart of Venice and "the finest drawing room in Europe") people everywhere were changing the kinds of places they inhabited, electronically extending themselves in whole new ways. And while the *Piazza di San Marco* (complete with everything but inhabitants) has been emulated at urban renewal sites across the United States, the hierarchy of importances from individual to monumental has vanished.

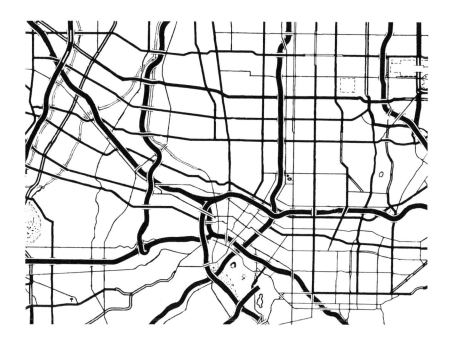

The Los Angeles freeway system

Industry went first. The pyramidal organization of the corporation has been replaced by networks much better suited to instant communication and instant feedback, allowing immediate response to daily market demands across enormous distribution systems, and forcing the early retirement of executives who cannot flexibly cope. The image of the pyramidal hierarchy — with someone or something clearly on top, and other successive layers of someone or something below that, sending their information to the apex and receiving orders back from on high — has vanished almost everywhere. The pyramids of business, like the pyramids of Gizeh, were built to last without any further help from anybody; the network, on the contrary, needs help. It needs to be plugged in — to the right markets to make money, to electricity in order to light up, to a sewage system in order to drain, and to a working social framework to avoid immediate malfunction.

For some time, the modern city (like the modern corporation) has been a model of the new "unhierarchy." Los Angeles, for instance, has poured itself unhierarchically across the landscape, demonstrating that you can now do almost anything you need to do in a city almost anywhere. It is curious to note with what consistency architects, and especially architecture students, continue to fly in the face of all the available facts. They breathlessly announce that the only problem worth their consideration is the super-high-density pedestrian urban core of the sort which continues to exist in New York, Calcutta, Province-

53

town, Carmel, and a diminishing list of other places (as though even problems were neatly ordered in a pyramidal hierarchy).

Archigram, a current British version of this old-fashioned systematizing, which was collected under the appellation "plug-in" and garnished with some handsome drawings, deserves special mention. It comes across as an arrangement that is really quite up-to-the-minute, in spite of the difficulties of giving credibility to an array of late-Victorian linear piping systems which would have put a gleam in the eye of Captain Nemo as he twiddled the valves of the *Nautilus*. All right, Archigram is very dense — but it seems to be based on the stage of the Industrial Revolution when mechanization meant repetition (a stage which even Detroit seems to have gotten through) so that those pretty, lumpy things seem odd survivors in an aspatial electronic world.

Where, then, does this leave us? What, if anything, can architects (place-makers) do? In an electronic world where space and location have so little functional meaning, there seems little point in defining cities spatially, even in the negative terms devised by those scholars who postulate hollow honeycombs with crowded edges after center cities are deserted. In a world which has lately witnessed the death of the old hierarchies, except in the aforementioned areas of resistance, it seems less than germane to consider new environments in terms of hierarchy. It seems less than essential as well to expose for demolition all the false ideologies in order to leave only the one true architecture (electric

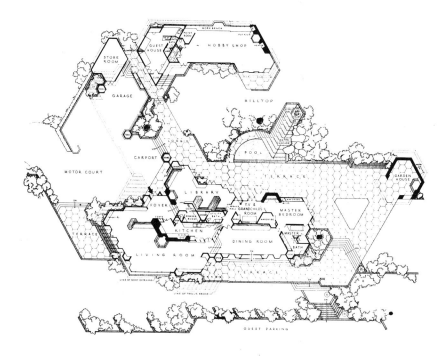

The Hanna house, by Frank Lloyd Wright

architecture) on its feet — particularly since there probably are not any good examples of it anyway.

Even at this early point in the new age, we can note that the architecture of the past several decades has not gained control of the physical environment. This architecture can accurately be called the architecture of exclusion. The perfectly natural attempts of the last several decades to find order by excluding disorder, and, by organizing whatever fragment remains into a system, is the order which characterizes it: for instance, Frank Lloyd Wright's Hanna house, where everything is thrown out that does not fit the organic geometry of the hexagon, into whose shape even bedsheets are somehow folded. If we can presume that the point of organic order is to make something with a life which somehow grows, reproduces itself, and spreads into other aspects of life, then sadly we have to admit that the Hanna house has spawned no progeny. The very specialness and difficulty of twisting and shoving everything into a geometry so natural for bees (and so awkward for us) leave the architect with a lovely geometry which stands apart from everything — and everything else seems to have the edge. Similarly, Ludwig Mies van der Rohe's geometry at the Illinois Institute of Technology excluded the possibilities not inherent in the 18 by 24 foot rectangular grid from which his campus plan started. This geometry has the extra attribute of being almost undiscoverable by anyone on the ground who is not simultaneously looking at a plan drawing.

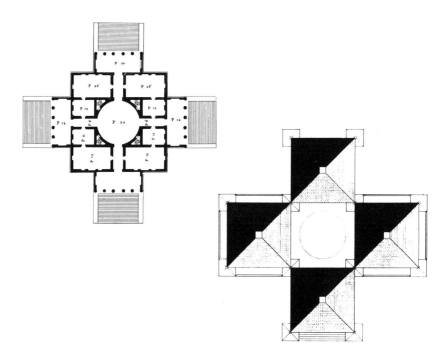

The Villa Rotonda, by Andrea Palladio (above left)
Trenton Bath Houses, by Louis I. Kahn (above right)

Andrea Palladio's designs, which sought to achieve with geometric order the harmony of the spheres, were more than empty games. They were central to the thought of their generation in all the arts, from logic to music. The same geometries applied to achieve four-way axialities on the dunes of East Hampton seem to have failed at bringing the whole culture around.

Nonetheless, the assumption that geometry has not solved the environment problems of twentieth-century design is given the lie by the work of Louis I. Kahn. His geometries begin as formally as Wright's or Mies's or even Palladio's, but his happiest moments seemed to occur in the primitive mass masonry of Pakistan or India. His formal enthusiasms appeared to be contemporary with those of the Baths of Caracalla, but he cleared the way, and served as the guide for most of the includers whom I now propose (and he stayed ahead of them too).

The architects of exclusion have for decades been perfecting their art, and they have built buildings on the plots assigned them. But somehow the commercial strip, which they abhor, has arrogated to itself more vitality, more power of growth, indeed more *inevitability* of growth, than the whole of their tidy output put together.

The manifestation of all this vitality must have some message for us. I doubt that the message is just that the architect who produces at enormous expense a replica of the commercial strip is about to save the world. But it does

A commercial strip in Los Angeles

seem reasonable, after the long failure by architects of exclusion to come to grips with our civilization, that the chance should now be seized by architects of inclusion. They can make their order with as much of life as they can include, rather than with as little. They welcome redundancy and depend on it, even as the electronic information networks do. They are willing to accept into their own systems of organization those ambiguities and conflicts of which life is made.

Robert Venturi's[2] search for ambiguity is probably the clearest instance of a conscious architecture of inclusion. His interests range from the history of architectural composition (with an encyclopedic knowledge of its hallowed monuments) to the popular roadside manifestations of our own time. His Guild House for the elderly in Philadelphia calls at once upon the intricacies of apartment floor-planning of the 1920s and the simple palette of materials of nineteenth-century Philadelphia. To these is added a kind of commercial formalism with a row of white subway tile, which makes a gesture toward the grandest kind of historical composition — dividing the whole big lump of a building into base (of white tiles), shaft (of brick), and capital (of brick as well, but divided from the shaft by the course of white tile). Without ever departing from homely matter-of-factness, a gold-anodized television antenna provides a sculptural flourish at once fiercely ingenious and pathetic (we know how cheap they are). Directly below this flourish the conflicting requirements of entrance and

Guild House in Philadelphia, by Robert Venturi (above)
Whitney Avenue Fire Station in New Haven, by Peter Millard (opposite)

central support fight it out. On the back of the building, the unadorned bricks and apparently regular holes state confidently that this is an ordinary housing project.

The Whitney Avenue firehouse in New Haven, by Peter Millard, has meticulously toilet-trained pipes and conduits, and appears at first to have little in common with its gaudier sisters of the strip. Yet the architect's attempt to include things, to worry about conflicts which need to be demonstrated and more problems which need to be solved, all involve him in the complexities of his problem with the same intensity with which Venturi's buildings take on the problems that beset them.

It is a special pleasure to give notice to a building (with no architect of record) which is a particularly moving example of the architecture of inclusion. The Madonna Inn, on the highway south of San Luis Obispo, California, would never get a passing grade in a school of architecture where tastefulness was prized. It was built (and keeps being built) by a family of highway contractors named Madonna, whose involvement with bulldozers and enormous pieces of earth-moving equipment puts them in close touch with huge boulders, which they have, with enormous feeling, piled together to make a motel, restaurant, and gas station. Entry into this motel, past a rock and down a stair into a dining room upholstered in purple velvet, is one of the most surprising (and surprisingly full) experiences to be found along an American highway.

The Madonna Inn near San Luis Obispo, California

It may be beside the point (but I don't think so) that in the men's room, next to a giant shell with gold faucets, the approach to a great rock grotto, which serves as a urinal, interrupts the beam of an electric eye and sets going a waterfall down over that grotto. It is disquieting, in another way, to note that armies of Italian craftsmen are even today meticulously carving grapes into wooden capitals and beating sheets of copper into shape over tables in the coffee shop. It is not at all disquieting, but rather exhilarating, to note that here there is everything instead of nothing. There is a kind of immediate involvement with the site, with the user and his movements, indeed with everything all at once, with the vitality and vulgarity of real commerce. It quivers at a pitch of excitement which presages, more clearly than any tidy, sparse geometry, an architecture for the electric present.

C.M.

The Minneapolis Federal Reserve Bank:
Looking in the gift horse's mouth

The Michigan architectural firm of Gunnar Birkerts and Associates has achieved a major reputation for their abiding interest in clear and powerful architectural shapes that make startling structural declarations. And their design for the Federal Reserve Bank of Minneapolis is certainly, by those standards, an impressive realization of impressive aims. There it is — big, bold, and real, the product of the enthusiasm and imagination of the architects, the engineers, and the client.

The architects took a complicated program and rendered it in absolutely vivid and unforgettable terms. The Bank's secure areas (about 60 per cent of the total) are put below ground underneath a sloping plaza. Clerical and administrative operations are housed in a shimmering glass office block that spans the gap between two great concrete towers, and is supported, like a suspension bridge, by two sturdy "catenary" members (so called because the shape of their curve is that made by a chain — *cadena* — hanging freely between two points). The curve is also echoed in the curtain wall of the facades; below it, the glass stands forward, and above it stands behind. The whole effect of the design is striking because it is so eminently clear. Ask anybody in Minneapolis about the Federal Reserve building; if they draw a blank, then describe a catenary curve with your hand, and they will know what you mean. This fact in itself represents an achievement of sorts.

The architects' design commanded a remarkable performance from the

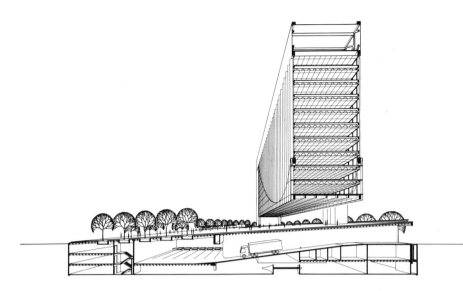

Section through the Federal Reserve Bank (above)
The Federal Reserve Bank of Minneapolis, by Gunnar Birkerts and Associates (opposite)

structural engineers. Most of them knew that it was possible to build an office building with a column-free span of 275 feet, but few had actually done it. and few would quibble over the reported price tag of about $47 a square foot. In concept, the structure is simplicity itself. Two catenaries, one on either side of the building and 60 feet apart, support the two major facades; the top part of each facade rests on the catenary, and the bottom part hangs from it. The facades are in turn rigid frames which support the 11 floors that span between them. The tendency of the supporting towers at either end of the building to topple inward is checked by two 28-foot deep trusses at the top, and the space in between them contains the mechanical equipment.

One result of all these labors by the architects and engineers is a set of eminently flexible work spaces, not broken up by interior supporting walls or cores. Another result is the creation of a two-and-a-half-acre public plaza — a "gift" to the people from the Federal Reserve Bank.

The original Minneapolis Federal Reserve was, like many other banks everywhere, a windowless, forbidding structure whose architect, Cass Gilbert, described it as a "strongbox for the currency of the Northwest." The president of the Bank today echoes Gilbert's concern for security (there is a heliport on the roof for hasty evacuation), but he also adds a new twist: "The responsibility of the Bank to serve the financial community and the public requires openness and accessibility." This may indeed seem an admirable intention,

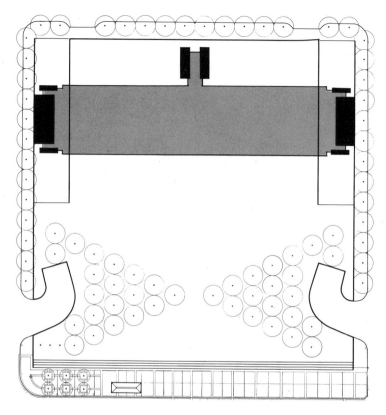

Proposal for Tougaloo College in Tougaloo, Mississippi, by Gunnar Birkerts and Associates (above)
Plan of the Federal Reserve Bank (opposite top)
Facade of the Federal Reserve Bank (opposite bottom)

resulting in offices with a view, and a plaza for the general public amusement. Admirable, too, may be the intentions behind the unabashedly glamorous form of the bank and the unusual structural system.

So with such good intentions, realized within several sets of real constraints, it is not unfair to ask this question: just what, in fact, has been achieved?

One thing that has at least been attempted is something that was not necessarily in the program to begin with, but which has nevertheless concerned the architects for a number of years. This is their notion of the "layered city." They maintain that many modern cities fail to achieve complete success as designs because they are zoned horizontally. The central business district forms one zone; the cultural center, the medical center, the shopping centers and the residential districts form other more or less discrete zones. Their location demands a great deal of transportation of goods and people from one place to another, creating at least some of the practical problems which most major cities now face. Thus the architects propose an alternative system in which the various zones are integrated in horizontal layers.

Their campus plan for Tougaloo College in Mississippi, for instance, has three layers. The bottom one has a traffic loop and scattered parking lots which fit under the buildings. Thus goods and services and people can be delivered (or can deliver themselves) to the buildings from below. The next layer is the "academic matrix;" the planning principle here is a kind of finger system and

Model of the ultimate phase of the Federal Reserve Bank

by the addition of units to the fingers future space requirements can be accomodated. Above the academic matrix are the dormitories, connected to the middle layer by stairs and walkways. By being superimposed, they are meant to be more integrated than if they were spread out horizontally into separate zones.

The architects liken this arrangement to that of medieval cities, where activities were interlocked in close proximity to each other. The comparison is certainly apt, as is their concern for what happens to a city when everything is divided up into neat and separate zones — a problem we describe in a later chapter (pages 131-142). What they propose, though, looks discouragingly like just another version of the same thing — a vertical zoning rather than a horizontal one. And in fact many modern cities, notably Manhattan, are already layered in this fashion anyway, with many of the services underground, stores and shops and sidewalks at ground level, and offices and apartments above. The architects propose to extend such existing arrangements further by putting *all* transportation and services underground, reserving the ground for pedestrian traffic, recreation, and commercial activities. Residential and office space would, again, be above.

The Federal Reserve Bank of Minneapolis is, in the architect's minds, (and perhaps to the astonishment of the client) one part of a layered city. It is designed to be expanded either upward or outward across an entire city, though it is not completely clear how such an expansion could be imposed upon an exist-

Proposal for a "layered city"

ing city without some major political and social readjustments. Problematical, too, is the question of whether or not the specter of giant buildings leaping across freeways would inspire pleasure and awe — or simply strike terror into the hearts of the citizens of Detroit, which is the subject of the architects' experiment shown in the photograph above.

In any case, whatever excitement could possibly be generated by a building hanging above a highway brings us straight to the major disappointment of the Federal Reserve Bank of Minneapolis. It is dramatically spanning something that very evidently does not need spanning. The architects assert that the security area below, with its complicated arrangement of vaults and service ramps, made a conventional column system difficult to use, if not impossible — though such problems have been solved before in conventional ways. They also assert that hanging the office part of the Bank above the ground allows them to give back virtually *all* of the site to the people. This act is consonant with the Bank officials' stated desire to make a gesture of openness to the city.

Assuming for the moment that such a statement is not mere public relations hype (and that there is in fact some conceivable reason why a bank — particularly one that holds no commercial or personal accounts — should seem open and accessible), it is worth asking what has really been given back to the people. A plaza, of course, and a very big one. It is equipped with a fountain, seats, planting, sculpture, electrical and television outlets, and provisions for

Plaza of the Federal Reserve Bank

a temporary stage — all there to induce several kinds of public use.

But one wonders whether these events won't have to be programmed, rather than occuring spontaneously — that is, whether they will not be infrequent rather than frequent. Since the plaza slopes up to a point high above the street on one side, it does not invite, or indeed even allow, a flow of pedestrian traffic across it. Since the entrance to the Bank is not from the plaza, but from the street below, not even the people who go into it cross the plaza automatically. Since it is altogether unprotected by surrounding buildings, people who do use the plaza are likely to find it uncomfortable on those frequent occasions in Minneapolis when the mercury dips below zero. One bank employee even quibbled that it was uncomfortable in the summer, when he tried to eat his lunch there: the big, black steel tubes that serve for public benches were too hot to sit on, and when he sat down on the granite his boiled egg rolled away from him. "He can always find another seat in the shade," the architect retorted. *Qu'ils mangent de la brioche?*

If the plaza is indeed uncomfortable or unfriendly, then there are bound to be reasons for it more serious and more instructive than the capricious escape of a boiled egg. These reasons lie in the realms of scale and shape.

In the first place, all of the parts seem either very large (the building and the surface of the plaza itself) or very small (the benches, sculptures, trees, and people). There is very little to mediate between the largeness and the smallness,

The Federal Reserve Bank, seen from the side opposite the plaza

to soften the blow of the Bank's dramatic facade while still maintaining its excitement. In this respect, the plaza is in strong contrast to the famous plaza at Rockefeller Center (which is described on pages 95-104) where a series of trees, sculptures, flagpoles, and smaller buildings carry the eye step by step upward to the RCA Building, itself stepped up in a series of vertical slabs seen dramatically from their thin sides.

In the second place, almost all of the elements in the plaza of the Federal Reserve Bank of Minneapolis are abstract. The benches there provide examples. Can sedentary happiness be found on a bench made out of steel tubing that looks like two big inner tubes? More generally, can the human imagination find comfort in an environment devoid of human connotation — in a facade that expresses a phenomenon of physics (the catenary curve) more than the human acts of being enclosed (by a wall) or looking out (through a window)?

What it unfortunately seems to come to here is that the architects, with all of their considerable talents, seem to have been responding as much to their own formal visions of architecture and of urban planning as to the dimensions of the real problem at hand. The energy, indeed the passion, of their response is everywhere evident, and they deserve great credit for their attempt to begin to see human needs in terms of large scale plans and monumental architectural forms. As we describe later in the chapter called "Modesty," we need those talents — once we find ways of really implementing large plans, and once

Sculpture and benches in the plaza of the Federal Reserve Bank

we can achieve some general agreement about what deserves monuments. For now the questions of what is possible and what, in that limited framework, is human seem a good deal more urgent.

G.A.

Two Buildings by Joseph Esherick:
Dedicated to the moving inhabitant, not the maker of form

It was supposed for a while in the 1960s that Ghirardelli Square in San Francisco carried to its limit the distance one could go in the sunny realm of urban design. Then came the Cannery.

The idea originated with a San Francisco lawyer, Leonard Martin, who conceived of the giant old Del Monte Cannery just behind Fisherman's Wharf as a natural setting for swank merchandisers. Martin's idea, in turn, was transmuted by architect Joseph Esherick into a phenomenon which seems to have a closer relationship to the Japanese tea ceremony (in its high period) than it does to Ghirardelli Square's more casual blandishments.

The warehouse is now transformed into a transportation museum, and the old railroad sidings have been turned into an olive grove. The Cannery itself was gutted, and only the old walls were left; inside these walls were placed three stories of brand new phenomena, split by a zig-zag pedestrian space. This space seems to shrug off any spatial crescendo. Instead, the people, busily buying expensive things on three levels, are the center of concern, forcing their powerful suggestion onto the newcomer who has not yet spent his money.

A curiously underplayed escalator and a dazzling elevator, as well as many stairs, entice people to where extraordinary architectural wonders lie.

The best things are the most nimbly flat-footed, like the plain pipe racks in the elegant men's shop or the lighting fixtures illuminating the sausages. The guest (to return to the tea ceremony) might feel the same queasiness that

Shop windows in the Cannery (above)
The Cannery in San Francisco, by Esherick Homsey Dodge and Davis (opposite)

he would in front of an ordinary thousand-dollar teapot as he views the straight-faced ritual combination of three hideous wallpapers in that very successful place called Spendiferous. He might or might not be taken aback on learning that the success of this establishment precipitated the advent of another apparel shop called Very Very Terry Jerry.

But it is, of course, the brick walls themselves that form the real bowl of tea, describing the game while they spin a narrative at once so dewy-eyed and so mad that a giant Byzantine fantasy becomes an elegant ingratiation. What is this tale the walls are telling? Will the sardines ever come back to be canned?

The notions of *wabi* and *sabi*, central to the ceremonial art of the Japanese tea masters during the last 400 years, are locked tight into the Cannery. These notions are based on the expectation that the humblest details of common life, and the objects that pertain to it, can after serious-minded study undergo a transfiguration which lifts them into the highest and purest levels of art. This is almost the opposite of Pop doctrine, which holds that if you can't beat 'em, join 'em. In seventeenth-century Japan, objects useful for the tea ceremony (like pots) might seem pretty ordinary to the uninitiated; they had the trans-muted quintessence of commonness. But these objects were so prized by con-noisseurs that they might bring a fortune in the marketplace, before taking a central role in a highly developed, highly esoteric, and certainly not popular ritual.

Sign over main entrance to the Cannery (above)
The Cannery interior (opposite top left)
Detail of hand rail in the Cannery (opposite top right)
Detail of the Cannery (opposite bottom)

I do not think it is altogether ridiculous to regard the transfiguration of the Cannery in rather the same light. In this case, Joseph Esherick is the tea master who possesses the key to the super-aristocratic ritual of understatement, while the many-wallpapered kitsch of the apparel shop called Spendiferous fills a role like that of the fabulous teapot.

To be sure, the pioneer tea master can occasionally be detected tripping over the stepping stones — or was he being pushed? The block-sized brick-walled ruins of the old Del Monte Cannery started to tell a narrative of white-walled pedestrian streets inside, where Esherick, who is the past-master of light slipping over white walls, could manipulate his magic; but then someone decided that all the plaster walls should be painted a spine-chilling, purply, almost-brick color which soaks up the light. This is a bit like burying the teapot.

A trip through the premises is very difficult to describe: It is so resolutely discursive (roughly like a Norse saga written by S. J. Perelman) that one comes away not exactly certain where he has been, or what this was. What it was, of course, was a Cannery (the old Del Monte Cannery), a brick-walled structure with repetitive gabled ends, occupying half a large block with railroad sidings separating it from a warehouse.

But the Cannery does not seem like a joke at all. This is serious play, like the tea ceremony was; and the very survival of the spirit of our cities, the transmutation of the local, the particular, and the common, to some sort of useful

74

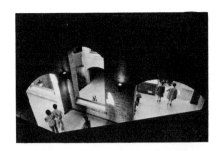

McLeod house in Belvedere, California by Esherick Homsey Dodge and Davis

universal is the prize. The ceremony is in the hands of a master; we can only hope that no one drops his cup.

With a house, even a fine Esherick house, the game is not so esoteric, nor are the dimensions so inscrutable. Here the architect's role, it seems to me, is less the tea master and more the action painter. At the McLeod house, on the top of Belvedere Island overlooking San Francisco Bay, there lingers the sense that the architect plunged down the steep hill past the oak trees to the marine view; he gobbled it all up and brought forth the house in chunks of light and outlook. This is the way the action painter flings his wet paint onto his canvas and then responds directly to it in whatever way the ensuing seconds seem to demand.

This is not to say that the McLeod house is careless. The detailing is meticulous, the workmanship neat, the range of materials and colors austerely disciplined, the strict budget carefully adhered to, and the attention to domestic comforts complete. It is just that the house maintains a permanent sense of exploding into its site.

The explosion is so casual, so easy to take, that Mrs. McLeod doesn't notice it any more, until she goes to anyone else's house and feels imprisoned. The house is probably this easy to take because it is not an explosion that consists of shapes crashing into other shapes, but of light, cushioned against the out-of-doors.

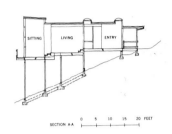

SECTION A A   0 5 10 15 20 FEET

McLeod house

The entry hall is already unexpectedly light, because of the skylight above the front doors. Another skylight is overhead at the first crossing point of action, where the two-by-four decking takes off downward, down the hall to the left, to vanish in light at a white wall beyond the stairs.

There is, however, scarcely time at first to grasp all this, because the floor is opening downward to the living room. There are views down the hill to the bay unfolding to the left, to the right, and ahead — heavily reinforcing the sense of downward motion. It seems limitless and beyond exploring, but is actually just some six risers' worth.

The movement does not end in the sitting room. From there the skylights, the high dining room ceiling, and the high glass onto the dining room deck — even the curious, inverse little bays between the sitting room and the living room — explode the house back up the hill. The sidewise opening of space up from the living room is especially memorable, over a cabinet past the higher dining room to a trellis and a great oak tree.

All this works so well, perhaps, because there isn't any "design," if design means making objects with agressive shapes. There are white walls, and soft warm walls of resawn redwood; there is a wood deck above, whose two by fours show; there are wood floors with a few soft oriental rugs; there is a simple fireplace; there are some standard floodlights which shine onto the white-painted walls.

77

Interior of the McLeod house

And there are lots of windows and skylights giving onto the site, each put there to respond to a special need, but each conceived as part of a more general requirement that is kinetic rather than static: dedicated to the moving inhabitant and not to the maker of form.

C.M.

Hadrian's Villa: A whole world in a circle and a square

Entrance to Hadrian's Villa at Tivoli is usually made against a stream of tourists pouring out looking very hot (if it is the season) and very tired (always), muttering, if they still have the strength, about how stupefyingly big it all was. It turns out, a few hundred yards later, that they were right; for sheer exhausting extent, rendered infinite by the blazing sun, the place has no peer. And yet architects flock to it, fascinated. This account is meant to examine what we see there, or perhaps what we think we see, in areas whose ruin is nearly complete, in order to try to find out why the villa has the meaning it has for us as twentieth-century architects. This is not meant to be an historical account; but one personality so dominates the place, and so affects our reaction to it, that any account must start with him. The villa still is very much Hadrian's.

A classmate of mine whose experiences I found awesome once noted that he was revolted by perversions to which he was not addicted. Similarly, we are likely to be fascinated when someone else's vagaries coincide with our own, however repellent they may seem. Ancient Romans are forever trotted out as worthy of our attention because they were, for ancients, so incredibly American. What is worse is that the comparison seems to hold up in detail to a point which encourages us to extend it even farther. Hadrian met with the Parthian king in a successful attempt to avert a war in an atmosphere which has a remarkably twentieth-century air. And even a comparison between Hadrian and his villa and Thomas Jefferson and his may not prove too far-fetched — though Hadrian, to be sure, is something of an enigma.

He has the reputation of having been a splendid sort for a Roman emperor, able and efficient, in possession of most of the qualities valued by nineteenth-century members of the British Liberal Party. But we also hear that he was especially interested in having himself worshipped as a diety (not very good form) and that his efforts to this end were remarkably successful in the eastern portions of his empire. His zeal, too, to deify his favorite, Antinous, after that young man had evaded the problems of aging by drowning in the Nile would strike us as even worse form in a Victorian. But the size of his undertakings, the avidity of his search for culture, and the gold-plated quality of his success at finding it are nothing short of Texan. And the sheer endlessness of his construction at Tivoli outdistances Versailles (which was, after all, based on a fairly simple idea) and competes with the scale of the twentieth century. The ruins of the General Motors Technical Center will be equally exhausting to walk among, though very probably not nearly so much fun.

Hadrian's entry in the megalomania division, though, since it bears so heavily the stamp of one man, seems much closer to the edge of madness. It is the product, as Eleanor Clark[1] pointed out, of a craze to build, very like those nineteenth-century follies in the United States whose owners, obeying only the dictates of some irresistible inner urge, added crazily, continually to them, and were generally stopped only by death. But this is not crazy in quite the same way, because this is often beautiful. It is perhaps more parallel with Thomas

Jefferson's efforts at Monticello, the work of a man moved to establish himself firmly on a piece of land, and to reaffirm the establishment by building there constantly, while his duties and his interests kept him far abroad. For Hadrian's conduct of his office, rather like John Foster Dulles's (or Henry Kissinger's), was based on travel. He strengthened the Roman Empire by traveling through it and formed his own character along the way. He had been born in Spain, but Athens was said to be his favorite place, and the art of Greece, some of it already over five centuries old, was his ideal — though he collected art from Egypt and the East, and many other places too, and he seems to have found the vaguely oriental charms of a Bithynian more to his taste than whatever Greek talent was available.

Indeed, the most striking point of rapport between Hadrian and ourselves is this eclecticism. Eclectic has been a dirty word for most of the twentieth-century. It is very recently, if yet, that most Modern architects have been willing to drop the pretense that their work springs to life full-blown from their un-influenced imaginations — or that it is the product of a new tradition, a twentieth-century version of a medieval craft. A medieval craftsman could work within his tradition, developing it unmindful of the work of other times and other places. A Renaissance man could form his images from Roman antiquity, as well as from local tradition, and nineteenth-century designers succumbed to the lure of a variety of rediscovered manners of building, which they sought to reproduce.

Model of Hadrian's Villa, with a view of the Canopus

But Hadrian was in another boat, very like our own. We are treated, every time we sit in a subway car and look at the ads above the windows, to maybe 30 different kinds of appeal — from abstractions in the manner of Mondrian on behalf of a bank, on past figures shaped like Life Savers or cigarettes, to a delicate line, vaguely Botticellian, which outlines a lady left clean and delicate by the right kind of shampoo. What is more, we respond to all of them. Books and magazines, movies, television, and easy travel flood our mind's eye with an incredible array of things. We could not shut them out, even if we wanted to, nor can we pick among them. Instead we have to transform them in our visions, absorb them into our whole selves, and then create, not from a fragment of our experience, but from the whole thing.

It is Hadrian's triumph that he did just this. He created at Tivoli, his biographer Spartian[2] says, representations of celebrated buildings and localities which had impressed him on his extensive travels. But he did not reproduce them into a Disneyland of exotic forms. He transformed them. Not only are they all Roman, they are a whole new kind of Roman style — less Greek, if anything, than what had gone on in Rome before. The orders and the marble revetments which were once applied to portions of the masonry forms are, to be sure, gone now, but they could never have been the whole show. There is too much excitement in the masonry forms themselves, in walls and vaults and especially in domes, and in spaces that must once have been domed. Behind

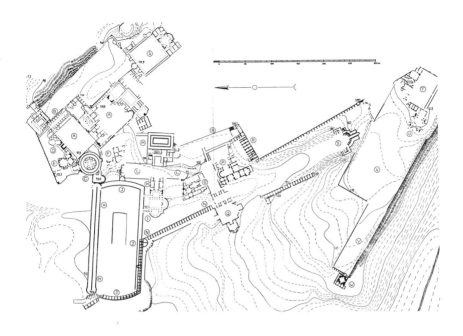

Plan of Hadrian's Villa

it all is the search for order in geometry.

Circles and squares, and a riot of combinations of the two, are the ordering devices which bring unity and continuity to the whole place. They are additive — as indeed we would expect from a complex that was constantly and obsessively added onto. It is not the sort of place which insists that nothing could be added or nothing taken away. That sort of complex would have been done in by several centuries of use as a quarry. But it is not, as far as we can tell, the sort of place subtly keyed to the various dictates of function. Countless hours have been whiled away by archaeologists assigning uses to the spaces and guessing what specific, exotic locale they were meant to recreate. But the archaeologists cannot agree, because the spaces are not thus specific. To take the terms from Louis I. Kahn, the villa is a realm of spaces, designed as spaces, domed and colonnaded, and made to evoke their use. The use, to take it from E. Baldwin Smith, would have been for the solemn palace ceremonies based on those of the Hellenistic east which deified Hadrian — in the setting of the royal symbolism of the colonnade, the divine and celestial symbolism of the dome, and (I suspect) the fertility symbolism of flowing water. Professor Smith, who must often have been at Tivoli under the sun of noon, opined that "without the solemn formalities of a court ritual, which presented him as a manifest god, his architectural creations at Tivoli would have been as empty, meaningless, and tiresome to him as they are to the casual visitor who wanders aimlessly from one unused structure to another."[3]

Animating the spaces beyond what we can see today, or perhaps beyond what we can imagine, would have been the rush and splash of flowing water, which was everywhere. It is possible to trace its presence, but almost impossible even to surmise what special delights each fountain offered. Did some of them bubble, or jet up to support balls and dancing objects in the air, or splash in pretty rivulets? And did some quietly moisten mosaics, or lie still and mysterious in deep pools? Scholars have noted that a recurrent feature of the villa would have been long vistas down straight axes, along which there would have been alternate pools of light and shade, so that moving from one area to another would begin to be an ordered experience in time. The sight and sound of the water, and its flow, must have contributed even more to this processional quality, toward bringing some coherence into the passage from space to space. This coherence now, in the passage among the ruins, is of all qualities the most elusive.

The site for Hadrian's Villa in the foothills at the edge of the Roman *campagna* raises an immediate question: why would a man with an empire to choose from have picked this site? Jefferson chose for Monticello a hilltop which commanded the widest and most beautiful prospect he knew. The views from the town of Tivoli, not far above Hadrian's villa are magnificent. The weather is better, and surely the site was available to the emperor. Hadrian's view of the *campagna* does not extend quite so far as Rome, and is, whatever the enthusiasts write, totally unremarkable, while the Vale of Tempe, which lies between the villa and the mountains behind it, has been accurately described as a gulch. The gulch owes even its present size, it turns out, to excavations made there for material during the construction of the villa.

The *Touring Club Italiano* guidebook states, without conviction, that the unimpressive site was selected because the property belonged to Sabina, the wife who played such a negligible (or negative) part in Hadrian's life. That seems little enough reason, but then there was little enough reason for all the fuss over the Bithynian shepherd boy Antinous, who was bland and pudgy, sulky, and very probably quite brainless. It was the emperor's energies that turned him into a deity.

Perhaps it does not force the issue to suggest that the site below Tivoli was as tractable as Antinous, capable of being molded to the emperor's design, something fairly positive to start from, but capable of being swallowed up into the grand scheme. For here nature is dominated by geometry, more even than at Versailles. At Versailles a system of axes imposes a formal order on the grounds, but at Hadrian's villa there are no grounds, only the architecture which contains it all and includes spaces, roofed and unroofed, open to the outside and enclosed.

The mound which this architecture occupies, and must once have come

View of retaining walls with cubicles, by Giovanni Battista Piranesi

close to superseding, runs roughly north and south for almost a mile (though it seems longer) and is about a third that wide. To the east, beyond the so-called Vale of Tempe lie the Sabine mountains; to the west stretches the flat Roman *campagna*, visible almost to Rome, which is fifteen miles away. The villa wrapped around the north, west, and south sides of the mound, cut well below its surface in places, especially at the Canopus and the Inferi, and extended well past it in other places, notably the Poikele. There the hill has been superseded by a multi-storied wall filled with cubicles for guards or slaves. This retains a vast earth-terrace at a dizzy height above the slope — a lovers' leap, as someone has called it,[4] shored up on slave quarters. It all seems frightfully undemocratic, a horror mitigated for us, perhaps, because Jefferson did exactly the same thing on a much smaller scale at Monticello. There a semi-underground level of service rooms builds up the top of his hill and makes a base for the geometry of the pavilions he places above. At Tivoli the scale of the natural formations and of man-made structures coincides, so that the hills become in a sense man-made, and the structures take on the quality of a natural formation.

Some areas are named on the official plan, but this is in most cases for convenience only, and to commemorate the endless efforts of archaeologists to find places in the ruins to accord with the descriptions of Spartian, who related how the emperor "created in his villa at Tivoli a marvel of architecture and landscape-gardening; to its different parts he assigned the names of celebrated

Wall of the Stoa Poikele and apse of the "Hall of Philosophers"

buildings and localities, such as the Lyceum, the Academy, the Prytaneum, the Canopus, the Stoa Poikele, and The Vale of Tempe, while in order that nothing should be wanting he even constructed a representation of Tartarus."[5] A few places, especially the Canopus and the Stoa Poikele, are clear enough. The rest of the names at least facilitate discussion and recall how well these spaces defy labeling.

The modern entrance to the area is from the north, toward the Poikele. The ancient approach, supposed to have been via the Poikele and the Canopus, is the most satisfying place to imagine entering the villa itself, since the approach would have to pass under the huge retaining walls stuffed with rooms (the Hundred Chambers) which support the Poikele high above the slope of the hill. Entrance is into a vestibule big enough to celebrate the advent of the deified emperor, with a portico and a semicircular apse forcing the juxtaposition of a square and a circle, to set a theme around whose recurrence the geometry of the whole villa is organized.

Right from the vestibule, along the one long axis of the complex, lies the Canopus. The axis followed to the left would lead to the Poikele. And just across the axis, to the left and right lie two baths, variously labelled men's and women's or summer and winter or large and small. One of Piranesi's *Vedute di Roma*, of the larger baths, comes as close as any one drawing can to showing the excitement that attended the translation of Hadrian's two-dimensional

View of the larger baths, by Giovanni Battista Piranesi

circles and squares into a three-dimensional piling up of vaults and domes. Piranesi's splendid foliage creeping over the bared masonry doubtless pleases us more than the sumptuous materials that would once have covered the surfaces, although this is the area where some stucco decoration does survive, and it is very fine. During the century and a half which preceded Hadrian, the Romans had fallen into the habit of hanging their structures with fancy-dress systems of columnar decorations, generally banal enough, and very nineteenth-century. Poor Hadrian seems to have had even the same crosses to bear that we do, furnished by the taste of his predecessors. Pretty clearly, though, in such a place as these large baths, no cosmetic application could veil the clarity and strength of the simple geometry. It is a geometry that is immensely effective, capable of containing without dissolution huge quantities of bejewelled and polychromed jazz. To judge from the quantities of *objets d' art* found here and mercifully spirited away, Hadrian must have had his hands full, even so.

The Poikele is a huge colonnade, 330 feet by 750, suggested, we are told, by the Stoa Poikele, or "painted porch," in Athens. In spite of the general agreement about its name, it is hard to understand on architectural grounds. The orientation of this part of the villa, as we have seen, has been shifted from that of the Canopus and the baths, in response to the curve of the hill. This great field, perfectly level, leaves the hill, and soars to the west, out over the valley retained high above the slope by the Hundred Chambers. The magnitude

88

"Maritime Theater"

of all this undertaking is hard to realize from on top, and the need for a vast flat field right at this point is lost on us, though the power that comes from the simple geometric form is not. The shape, the same kind of rectangle with concave ends that we saw in the smaller baths, is echoed by a large pool in the center. Around that, some say, would have been a hippodrome, or, as it has been hypothetically restored, a garden. Around that is supposed to have been a kind of cloister, which would be less moving than the fragment left standing along the north side of the field. It is a great wall, 250 yards long and almost 10 yards high, which runs almost due east and west, so that the south side is in sun, and along the north is shade. The simple strength of this statement — a long slab surrounded by space, which divides sun from shade — amasses a grandeur which, in its ruined state, is more than just Roman.

   At the east end of this great wall, past the Hall of the Philosophers, is the circular area that makes a pivot point on the plan and is, more than any other single place, the focus and the heart of the villa. It is called the Maritime Theater, or the Natatorium. But neither of these names makes any sense. It is a round island, surrounded by a moat which is surrounded with a colonnade, which in turn is backed by a circular wall. In Hadrian's time, the island was reached only by two retractable bridges. As we have seen, in the villa water was used everywhere, creating with its flow an image of distance, creating an image of immersion. But here in this round place the water is made to create the image

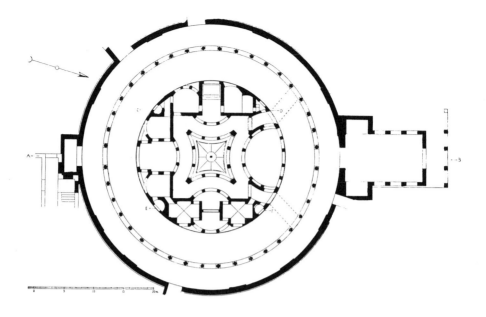

Plan of the "Maritime Theater"

of an island, with all the sense of withdrawal and independence that an island implies. Here in this vast jungle of ruins is an inviolate place, a perfect circle surrounded by water, with a stronger sense of place than anywhere else in the villa.

On the island are incredibly small rooms, and in the center of it all is a tiny atrium, square with concave sides, which must have held a fountain, a source of active moving water which would have lost itself in the still waters of the moat around. What went on in the rooms is anybody's guess, but it was surely something very special.

The concentric circles of island, moat, and colonnade make what seems like a pivot point in the plan. But two affairs called Libraries invite a set of spatial problems by continuing the direction of some structures south of the island into an area where everything is oriented in a new direction. The Ospidali, which occupy the adjacent side of the rectangular courtyard against which the Libraries are wedged, are shown as guest rooms. But it would take a peculiarly eccentric Texan to stuff his guests into cubbyholes like this, even though water channels there suggest heaven knows what sort of hidden delights.

(This is perhaps the time to point out that the hidden delights in all this mass of masonry have been poked among not only with archaeological skill that we would expect by now, but with skill and verve and high excitement by Eleanor Clark, in *Rome and a Villa*, and Marguerite Yourcenar[6], in *The*

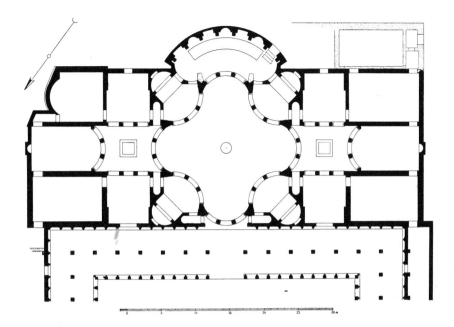

Plan of the Piazza d'Oro

Memoirs of Hadrian. Their own monuments are not to be sliced into, but must be taken all at once, like Hadrian's. Their fantasies, however, as well as their insights have become, as Piranesi's did earlier, a part of the place in the way that more recent residences gain fame for the guests they have sheltered. So their speculations appear here.)

On past endless rooms of the Imperial Palace, past the Hall of the Doric Pillars, lies the Piazza d'Oro, so grandly named because the objects taken from here were even more sumptuous than the ones from anywhere else. The Piazza itself is a rectangle, whose 68 columns were alternately of Oriental granite and *cippolino.* It is entered through the center of one short side through a vestibule which is octagonal, with alternate sides concave, so that it looks in plan like a square with rounded corners. It would have had a domical vault for the celectial implications of the ceremonies when the deified emperor arrived here. Flanking the vestibule, opening into the Piazza, are square vaulted spaces with half-circular niches. On one of the long sides of the Piazza, facing northeast, a half-round area faces the Vale of Tempe, but opposite the vestibule lies what must have been a space reserved for the most elevating ceremonies. In plan it is a large octagon, with sides alternately concave and convex, not walled, only suggested by arcades, as San Vitale in Ravenna was to have its form suggested four centuries later.

On the concave sides, splayed rectangles helped fill a square. On the side

91

View towards the Canopus and Serapeion

opposite the entrance, which was convex, the form was echoed by an apsidal wall concentric with the convex arcade bordering the octagon. The two remaining sides, at right angles to the entrance and the apse, gave onto rectangles whose ends were concave. These rectangles had no walls, but only arcades into still other spaces. It is a Baroque summation of the simpler geometries of the square and circle which the whole villa has developed. And it was alive with water, flowing from everywhere. The water used in the rest of the villa and the geometry of the rest of the villa must here have reached a ceremonial crescendo — though at the center of everything, hundreds of yards away, lies the island.

Along the great axis we previously followed north lies the Valley of Canopus, artificially cut into the tufa rock of the hill. This is one part of the villa whose special affinities are in little doubt. "Canopus," according to Strabo[7], "is a town 120 stadia from Alexandria . . . containing a highly revered temple of Serapis . . . . Troops of pilgrims descend the canal from Alexandria to celebrate the festivals of this goddess. The neighborhood of the temple swarms day and night with men and women, who spend the time in their boats dancing and singing with the most unbridled merriment, or find accommodation in the town of Canopus and there prosecute their orgies." Hadrian's Canopus, too, has cubicles along the sides of the valley and a temple of Serapis at the end of a panel of water.

The canal restored and filled with water, is not really a canal at all (and

Interior of the Serapeion

Hadrian could certainly have afforded a canal if he had wanted it, if need be with water running uphill). It is a pool, in one of the characteristic shapes of the villa, a rectangle with convex end. At its north end a colonnade, with architrave alternately flat and arched, has now been restored — a form new even to Rome, and unheard of in Egypt. Opposite it, the temple took on an even more remarkable form, a melon-domed circle sliced off at the front, with a plane which would have produced an arched opening divided with columns. From behind the circular space came a tunnel, alternately roofed and unroofed (therefore light and dark), through which a major source of water flowed and splashed in fountains. The look here is forward, not back. The festivals in this Canopus were said to copy Egyptian ones, but neither the building forms nor the plans were copies of anything.

The rest of the Villa, to the south, looks fascinating in the books, with a ravine cut into the rock in order to recall, it is said, the River Styx, and mysterious underground passages connecting it with other underground phenomena, including one named after Tartarus. But they are private property and not part of a visit, and anyway there has already been, on even the coolest days, enough. The row of eighteenth-century cypresses that leads away from the hill is beautiful, its shade is deliciously cool, and we will want refreshment. We will probably not remember to look back. It will be later, when we need refreshment of another sort, that we will want to look again at the whole hill made over, devoted to the primacy of forms and a serious game of space — a game based on the subtlest permutations of the possibilities inherent in a circle and a square, and transforming with a circle and a square the objects and impressions of a whole world.

C.M.

Likenesses

Rockefeller Plaza in New York and the Rockefeller Center buildings that surround it are so famous that they need very little description. Although they have been abominated by some — "a series of bad guesses, blind stabs, and grandiose inanities," Lewis Mumford[1] once wrote — they make a place that is fun to visit, friendly and comfortable to be in. As a result (and in reaction to our late-century disenchantment with the charms of Modern architecture) many people have come to think of Rockefeller Plaza as one of the most splendid urban creations of the twentieth century, designed long before the full arrival of the International Style on our shores. Why does Rockefeller Plaza seem so special? What are the likenesses it purveys, and what do they have to tell us about designing public places? Not surprisingly, the answers are not straight-forward.

Describing his proposal for the rebuilding of Copley Square in Boston, Robert Venturi wrote that an open plaza is "seldom appropriate for an American city today except as a convenience for pedestrians for diagonal short-cuts. Americans feel uncomfortable sitting in a square: they should be working at the office or home with the family looking at television[2]." People nevertheless do appear to like Rockefeller Plaza, and the key to their enthusiasm is bound to be that they do indeed feel comfortable being there — that they feel they are somewhere that is different from somewhere else, that it is okay for them to be there, and that there is something for them to do, an occupation for their minds

Rockefeller Plaza (above)
Rockefeller Center, by Reinhard & Hofmeister, Corbett Harrison & MacMurray, and Hood
& Fouilhoux (opposite)

and bodies and the chance even for flights of their imagination.

Rockefeller Plaza is remarkably small — about 200 feet on each side — for the impression it makes. It is surrounded on all four sides by buildings, and even the Promenade and the streets which lead into it enforce the sense of enclosure. Unless you stand on the sidewalk of one of the cross-town streets (in which case you are not really in the plaza) there are no vistas that are more than about a block and a half long. The smallness of the plaza and this sense of relative enclosure make it seem very different from most of the other places nearby. In fact, the sense it provides of being almost enclosed in an outdoor public space is virtually unique on the island on Manhattan, except for the lower part which was developed before the imposition of the grid plan of avenues and cross streets in 1811.

In addition to providing a sense of enclosure, Rockefeller Plaza has the fortune of being well populated. Many people seem anxious to run with the pack when faced with the large-scale anonymity of crowds in a city, and they become comfortable by becoming slightly anonymous themselves, by not attracting unwanted attention, and by not seeming idlers. Thus Rockefeller Plaza can attract people to it because of the number of people who automatically walk through it, providing a critical mass of population to signal that this is a place for people. People are almost never by themselves there, and neither is there a lack of some casual thing to be doing, just in case someone should,

97

Ornament and decoration around Rockefeller Plaza (above)
Rockefeller Center buildings seen from the center of the Plaza (opposite)

in fact, ask what they are doing. They are looking in shop windows, or at fountains or at flowers or at flags. If the season is right, they are looking at the skaters on the rink. There are, after all, plenty of other people doing the same things. The kind of sociability that develops here is pleasantly isolationist. Many people are in each other's presence, but not necessarily in each other's company. The plaza would seem like an unlikely place for a spontaneous public demonstration to swell up: it feels too small, too contained, too comfortable for that.

On the other hand, so many cozy amenities could make the place so pleasant, so polite that it might almost seem boring. Boring, however, it is not. For the eye and for the imagination there are no constraints. The thin slabs of the surrounding buildings, for instance, lead the eye upward to exhilarating heights. And the ornaments on the buildings and in the plaza itself lead the imagination away. Almost all of them use human figures in motion to embody some mythic phenomenon. Some of the figures have historical precedents — like Atlas or Prometheus or Mercury. Others were invented on the spot for the occasion — like Sound, above an entrance to the RCA Building. Together these figures populate the place with suggestions of human life, suggestions which may indeed be at least as vivid for the imagination as people themselves.

Rockefeller Plaza is semi-enclosed and comfortable; there are many pleasant things to do there, and exciting things to look at and to think about. Many of the qualities it possesses make it stand in strong contrast to most American

New Rockefeller Center buildings, seen from the Avenue of the Americas

plazas of more recent vintage — including, for instance, the barren and sometimes wind-swept expanse of granite in front of the Federal Reserve Bank of Minneapolis (pages 61-70) and, for that matter, the more Modern series of buildings across the Avenue of the Americas which make up the recent extension of Rockefeller Center.

New York's zoning regulations were revised in 1961 in a major attempt to use zoning incentives to achieve certain desired urban design goals. In partial compensation for cuts in the allowable size of buildings, the regulations permitted a developer an increase in floor area of up to 20 per cent if he provided a plaza, and a smaller bonus if he provided an arcade. Urban designer Jonathan Barnett has pointed out that the new zoning regulations had the effect of "belatedly imposing this concept of modernism on New York City, creating towers that stand in their individual pools of plaza space, surrounded by the party walls of earlier structures that were planned to face the street. Shopping frontages are interrupted, and open spaces appear at random, unrelated to topography, sunlight, or the design of the plaza across the way."[3] The extension of Rockefeller Center on the west side of the Avenue of the Americas responded directly to the 1961 zoning, and these buildings are well worth looking at, since they embody the latter-day plaza principle so clearly, since this principle has become almost automatic in other cities, and since it has now become fashionable to criticize it out of hand.

New Rockefeller Center buildings, seen from the plaza of the Mc-Graw-Hill Building

First, though these plazas in front of the New Rockefeller Center buildings may indeed feel inhuman — as some of their critics have claimed — they are certainly not unpeopled. The working population in their part of town is much too large for that, and the plazas are far too accessible. Thus we come to an obvious point: public spaces will be used if they are accessible, and if there are enough people around to make everyone feel easy about being there — and this will happen quite independently of the particular finesse which went into their design. Second, these plazas and the buildings that face them are not — as some people have hastily concluded — merely inept examples of architecture and urban design, though some of us may well not like them.

By all evidence, the plazas work very well, and, as importantly, the build-ings, seen without prejudice, make a powerful and perhaps even unique im-pression on the mind. Together they make a *place* in the city that is not the same as any other place. True, there is no sense of comfortable enclosure here, as there is at the original Rockefeller Plaza, and the buildings seem to make mini-mal accommodations to the street and the people on it; they simply crash into the ground. All of the imagery, too, is rigorously impersonal. The buildings around Rockefeller Plaza all have conventional double-hung windows, de-signed for natural ventilation before the advent of the hermetic ecosystems which now enclose most high-rise buildings. The conventional windows are recognizable as such, and our recognition is a function of their shape and their

The McGraw-Hill and Exxon buildings

scale. They are repeated over and over again up the faces of the tall buildings, and they carry with them the suggestion of human habitation inside. In the newer buildings, it is hard to recognize either shape or scale, hard to distinguish window from spandrel, or either of them from the tall vertical slits that run almost continuously from bottom to top. The suggestion of window is gone, and so is the suggestion of people. Similarly, whereas the decoration on the buildings in Rockefeller Plaza recalls and reproduces the human figure in motion, in the newer buildings the embellishments are all abstract — like the triangular sculpture in front of the McGraw-Hill Building.

So the effect of these buildings and their plazas is powerful, and it is expansive, impersonal, and abstract. The key to success here is that whatever these buildings are doing to the public space of the city, they are doing it together. They are unusual examples of their kind, because there are a number of them side by side, and they are all flanked by high-rise shafts designed to a similar format. Thus they are not breaking up an urban fabric. Whether or not we like it, they are weaving a fabric that is all their own.

The main lessons of the original Rockefeller Plaza and of the plazas in front of the newer Rockefeller Center buildings are not about style; they are about making places — or, for that matter, about making anything else worth having. You can take butter and flour and milk and make a béchamel sauce, or you can take oil and vinegar and herbs and make a vinaigrette. But vinegar

The RCA building

and milk don't make anything but a mess. A part of the problem is to know how to make what you want.

Another part of the problem, of course, is to realize that the repertory of things you can do is vast, and that you have many options in selecting those which seem worthwhile. For most architects, however, that realization has been fairly slow in coming. Most of them practicing today received their education since the Second World War, and a good part of their education came from the copybook of Modern architectural theory — which in its various chapters declared that ornament was a crime, that the historical styles were a lie, and that, as Walter Gropius once said, a breach had been made with the past. The teachings of the Modern movement represented an intentional attempt to sever what had gone before, and to create a new style — independent of history, based on logic, reflective of the technological civilization of the Modern age, and capable of achieving honesty of thought and feeling. The effort was not intended to accomodate the needs and visions of the present in some comfortable continuum of history, but to have it either/or: either Modern or old-fashioned, either okay or bunk. The effort was, in a word, revolutionary. They may have been right. They were certainly fervent, they were certainly doctrinaire, and they were certainly (in their revolutionary way) orthodox.

Unfortunately, we do not need orthodoxies like that. All of us every day face the onslaught of experiences which require varied, complex, and agile responses. This is to say that we inhabit a pluralist world, and that we ourselves are many-faceted creatures. Thus no single orthodoxy — including the single-minded return to copying buildings from the past — will do, no single set of forms and images to shape the environment we build for ourselves. The meaning of buildings like those around Rockefeller Plaza and the new ones along the Avenue of the Americas is that architecture can have many potent likenesses. The choice is altogether ours, and the task is to learn to cast our nets backwards in time — and outwards — to find what feels right for a given design problem, and what among the many options seems really worthwhile.

G.A.

You Have to Pay for the Public Life

In 1964 I set out to find examples of contemporary monumental architecture in California which functioned as a part of the urban scene. I thought I might discover that there is no contemporary monumental architecture there, or that there is no urban scene (except in a sector of San Francisco), or perhaps that both monumental architecture and the urban scene were missing. These suspicions were well founded; any discussion from California about monumental urban architecture was bound to be less about what we had than about what we had instead.

Any discussion of monumental architecture in its urban setting should proceed from a definition of what constitutes "monumental," and what "urban" means to us. The two adjectives are closely related: both of them involve the individual's giving up something (space or money or prominence or concern) to the public realm.

Monumentality must have to do with monuments. And a monument is an object whose function is to mark a *place*, either at that place's boundary or at its heart. There are, of course, private monuments, over such places as the graves of the obscure. But to merit our attention here, and to be of any interest to most of the people who view it, a monument must mark a place of more than private importance or interest. The act of marking is then a public act, and the act of recognition an expectable public act among the members of the society which possesses the place. Monumentality, considered this way, is not a product of compositional techniques (such as symmetry about several axes), or flamboyance of form, or even of conspicuous consumption of space, time, or money. It is, rather, a function of society's taking possession of, or agreeing upon, extraordinarily important places on the earth's surface, and of the society's celebrating their pre-eminence.

A version of this agreement and this celebration was developed by José Ortega y Gasset into a definition of urbanity itself. "The *urbs* or *polis*," he says, "starts by being an empty space, the *forum*, the *agora*, and all the rest is just a means of fixing that empty space, of limiting its outlines . . . The square, thanks to the walls which enclose it, is a portion of the countryside which turns its back on the rest, eliminates the rest, and sets itself up in opposition to it."[1]

Ortega y Gasset's product is the city, the urban unit based upon the Mediterranean open square, a politically as well as physically comprehensible unit that people used to be willing to die for. The process of achieving an urban focus is the same as that of achieving monumentality. It starts with the selection of a place which is to be of particular importance, and it continues when the inhabitants invest that place with the attributes of importance, such as edges, or some kind of marker. This process, the establishing of cities and the marking of important places, constitutes most of the physical part of establishing civilization. Charles Eames has made the point that the crux of this civilizing process is the giving up by individuals of something in order that the public realm may be enhanced. In the city, urban and monumental places, indeed urbanity and monumentality themselves, can occur only when something is given over to the public.

Some planners have a way of articulating their (private) discovery that the public body's chief concern is *people*. They then say, unrelatedly, that it is too bad the sprawling metropolis is so formless. It might well be that if the shibboleth about people were turned inside out, if planning efforts went toward enlarging people's concerns — and sacrifices — for the public realm, that the urban scene would more closely approach the planners' vision, and that the people would be better served.

The most evident thing about Los Angeles, especially, and the other new cities of the West, is that, in contrast to any of the traditions we have inherited, hardly anybody gives anything to the public realm. Instead, it is not at all clear what the public realm consists of, or even, for the time being, who needs it. What is clear is that civic amenities (of the sort architects think of as "monumental") which were highly regarded earlier in this century are of much less concern today.

A pointed example is the small city of Atascadero, which lies in a particularly handsome coastal valley between Los Angeles and San Francisco. It was first developed in the 1920s as a real-estate venture with heavy cultural overtones and extensive architectural amplification. Extraordinarily ambitious

Atascadero, California

"monumental" architecture popped up all over the townsite. Buildings of a vaguely Italian Romanesque persuasion with a Classic Revival touch, symmetrical about several axes, faced onto wide malls punctuated or terminated by Canovesque sculpture groups. The effect was undeniably grand, if a bit surreal, exploiting wide grassy vistas among the dense California oaks.

But there wasn't much of a town until the 1940s. Then, on the major mall (an elaborately sunken panel of irrigated green) came a gas station, and then another one, and more recently an elevated freeway has continued the destruction of the grand design. All this has happened during the very period in which Philadelphians, with staggering energy and expense, have been achieving in their Center City long malls, grand vistas at every scale, an architectural expression overwhelmingly serene, an urban desideratum which the Atascaderans did not especially want or need, and have been blithely liquidating. Does this liquidation not constitute some sort of crime against the public?

Before we start proceedings, we should consider what the public realm is, or rather, what it might be in California now and during the decades ahead. The "monumentality" and the "urbanity" that we seek may then be appropriate as functions of our society, and not of some other one.

In California cities, as in new cities all over the country, the pattern of buildings on the land is as standard as it is explosive. Everywhere near population centers, new little houses surrounded by incipient lawns appear. They could be said to be at the edge of the city, except that there is no real edge — thanks to the speed of growth, the leapfrogging of rural areas, and the long commercial fingers that follow the highways out farther than the houses have yet reached. Meanwhile, in areas not much older, houses are pulled down as soon as zoning regulations allow, to be replaced with apartments whose only amenity is a location near a garage in the basement.

The new houses are separate and private — islands, alongside which are moored the automobiles that take the inhabitants off to other places. It might be more useful and more accurate to note that the houses and the automobiles are very much alike, and that each is very like the mobile homes which share both their characteristics. All are fairly new, and their life span is short. All are quite standard, but have allowed their buyers the agonies of choice, demonstrating enough differences so that they can readily be identified during the period of ownership, and so that the sense of privacy is complete, in the car as well as in the house. This is privacy with at least psychic mobility. The houses are not tied down to any *place* much more than the trailer homes are, or the automobiles. They are adrift in the suburban sea, not so mobile as the cars, but just as unattached. They are not so much like islands alongside which the cars are moored as they are like little yachts, dwarfed by the great chrome-trimmed dinghies that seek their lee.

This is, after all, a floating world in which a floating population can

Marin County Civic Center, by Frank Lloyd Wright

island-hop with impunity; one need almost never go ashore. There are the drive-in banks, the drive-in movies, the drive-in shoe repair. There is even, in Marin County, Frank Lloyd Wright's drive-in Civic Center, a structure of major biographical and perhaps historical importance, about whose forms a great deal of surprisingly respectful comment has appeared. Here, for a county filling up with adjacent and increasingly indistinguishable suburban communities, quite without a major center, was going to be *the* center for civic activities. It was to be the public realm, one would have supposed, for which a number of public-spirited leaders in the community had fought long and hard.

It might have been, to continue our figure, a sort of dock to which the floating populace might come: monumental in that it marked a special place which was somewhere and which, for its importance, was civic if not urban. But instead of a dock for floating suburbanites, it is just another ship, much larger than most, to be sure, and presently beached (wedged, in fact) between two hills. It demands little of the people who float by, and gives them back little. It allows them to penetrate its interior from a point on its underside next to the delivery entrance, but further relations are discouraged, and lingering is most often the result of inability to find the exit.

This kind of placelessness has not always been characteristic. During the 1920s and into the 1930s, with what was doubtless an enormous assist from the Hollywood vision in the days of its greatest splendor, an architectural image

110

Arcade of the Fox-Arlington Theater, by Edwards, Plunkett and Howell

of California developed. It was exotic but specific, derivative but exhilaratingly free. It had something to do with Helen Hunt Jackson's *Ramona*, with the benign climate, with the splendor of the sites and their floral luxuriance, with the general availability of wood and stucco. It also had to do with the assurance, supplied by Hollywood, that appearances *did* matter, and the assumption that we, the inheritors of a hundred traditions, had our pick. What came of this was an architecture that owed something to Spain, very little to the people who were introducing the International Style, and a great deal to the movie camera's moving eye.

It seemed perfectly appropriate to the energetic citizens of Santa Barbara, for instance, that after their city had been devastated by an earthquake, it should rise again Spanish. The railroad roundhouse became a bull ring, the movie house a castle. Everywhere in the rebuilt town, the act of recalling another quite imaginary civilization created a new and powerful public realm. Out of this public act came the Santa Barbara County Courthouse (pages 41-50) certainly one of the most extraordinary public buildings in the United States. It did so much about sweeping the whole landscape up around it that one might have expected the really large-scale projects of the 1960s to catch even more of the grandeur of the place.

Whole new college campuses, for instance, which sprung magically out of fields across the state, surely presented unparalleled chances to order a public

Detail of a building on the Stanford University Campus, by Shepley, Rutan, and Coolidge

realm, to invest a place of public importance with the physical attributes of importance. Yet, by any standards, the clearest and strongest campus to be found in the state is still the old campus at Stanford, designed in Boston by Shepley, Rutan, and Coolidge, and built in the years just after 1887. The buildings in the old campus are H. H. Richardson warmed over (and cooled off again in the long passage from the architects' Boston kitchens); the gaudy mosaic facade of the chapel, the centerpiece of the composition, is an affront to the soft yellow stone surfaces around it. But the play of the local sunshine across the long arcades, the endlessly surprising development of interior spaces from big to small to big again, the excitement of a sensible framework that is strong and supple enough to include the most disparate academic activities — all combine to make this a complete and memorable place. Even though the surrounding countryside is not swept into the picture, as at Santa Barbara, at least there is an orchestration of spaces varied and complete enough to evoke a complex public use.

It is a place, however, that dates from the previous century, and this is a survey of our own times, times that have multiplied opportunities for spatial and functional orchestrations like the ones at Stanford and Santa Barbara. What, then, do we have?

During the years of California's growth, the extravagances of the landscape and of the settlers on it have suggested to many that straight opulence

San Francisco City Hall, by Bakewell and Brown

might create centers of the public realm. In this respect, three city halls clamor for attention. The San Francisco City Hall probably leads the list in sheer expensive grandeur; its expensiveness was, one gathers, as much a political as a physical phenomenon, but the grandeur is a manifestation of the highly developed *Beaux Arts* compositional skills of the architects, Bakewell and Brown. These great skills, though, have been curiously ineffectual in commending themselves to the public concern. It is a sobering experience, for instance, to stand in the towering space under the aggressively magnificent dome and to notice that hardly anyone looks up. And the development of the extensive and very formal civic center outside has had remarkably little effect on the growth of the downtown area, which has remained resolutely separate from all this architectural assertion. Surely a part of the failure to achieve an important public place here rests with the entirely abstract nature of the *Beaux Arts*'s earlier international style. It takes a major master, like Sir Edwin Lutyens at New Delhi, to lift this idiom out of the abstract and give some point to its being somewhere. The San Francisco City Hall demonstrates skill, but no such mastery; so the city is not specifically enriched by its being there. It could be anywhere.

Or almost anywhere. It could not easily be in Gilroy. A small garlic-farming community north of Salinas, Gilroy relied on a similar, if more relaxed, show of opulence in the building of its own city hall in 1905. An elaborateness,

Gilroy City Hall

of vaguely Flemish antecedent, served the town's desires; a truly remarkable array of whirls and volutes was concentrated here to signal the center of the public realm. But, alas, this concentration has not kept its hold on the public mind much more effectively than San Francisco's city hall has, and now this fancy pile is leading a precarious life as temporary headquarters for the town's Chamber of Commerce and police station.

The citizens of Los Angeles adopted a slightly different route to achieve importance for their city hall. In their wide horizontal sprawl of a city, they went *up* as far as seemed practical, and they organized their statutes so no other buildings could go higher. But economic pressure has mounted, and now commercial structures bulk larger on the skyline than the city hall. The Angeleno's vertical gesture should get some credit, in any case, for being a gesture — an attempt to make a center for a city which otherwise had none. As a formal gesture, it has even had some little hold on the public mind, although its popular image now involves a familiar tower rising in the smoggy background while a freeway interchange fills the sharp foreground.

Thus the opulence and the effort involved in the San Francisco, Gilroy, and Los Angeles City halls both seem to come to very little in the public mind, lacking as they all do any activity which elicits public participation. Whatever the nature of the welfare state, these public buildings seem to offer far less to the passer-by than such typical — and remarkable — California institutions

114

as the Nut Tree, a roadside restaurant on the highway from Sacramento to San Francisco, which offers in the middle of a bucolic area such comforts as a miniature railroad, an airport, an extensive toy shop, highly sophisticated gifts and notions, a small bar serving imported beers and cheeses, a heartily elegant — and expensive — restaurant, exhibitions of paintings and crafts, and even an aviary — all of them surrounded and presented with graphic design of consummate sophistication and great flair. This is entirely a commercial venture, but judging from the crowds, it offers the traveler a gift of great importance. It is an offering of urbanity, of sophistication and chic, a kind of foretaste, for those bound west, of the urban joys of San Francisco.

In the days before television, moving-picture theaters afforded one of the clearest and easiest ways for people to participate in the American Dream. In Southern California, where movies came from, and where the climate allowed forecourts for theaters to be largely out of doors, some of the most image-filled places for the public to congregate were movie theaters. The Fox-Arlington Theater in Santa Barbara invites our inspection. The idiom is movieland Spanish (like nothing in Spain). The architectural opportunity was a double one. First, it was to make of the immense auditorium, set a block back from the theater's entrance on the main street, one of the city's noblest bastions, with high white walls sprouting turrets and balconies and follies. Only the grandest of the grandees of the other hemisphere could have afforded walls this size to

Tower of the Fox-Arlington Theater

stick their balconies onto. Second, and more importantly for the city, it was to make partly roofed and partly open the block-long passageway from the box office to the ticket-taker, thus providing the opportunity to extend the sidewalks of the city, still outdoors, past gardens and along a tiled esplanade, where soft lights play at night, and where by day the sun filters down among the leaves. Santa Barbara's sidewalks are ordinary enough, but in the mind's eye they merge with the passage to the Fox-Arlington Theater and other commercial arcades and patios off State Street to form a public realm filled with architectural nuance and, even more importantly, filled with the public.

Another such public monument, which should not soon be forgotten although it has been left isolated by Los Angeles' swiftly changing patterns is Grauman's Chinese Theater. It seems more astonishingly grand today than it did in the days when millions in their neighborhood theaters watched movie stars immortalizing bits of its wet concrete with their hands and feet.

To more recent times there are monuments as well. Indeed, by almost any conceivable method of evaluation that does not exclude the public, Disneyland must be regarded as the most important single piece of construction in the West in the past several decades. The assumption, inevitably made by people who have not yet been there, is that it is some sort of physical extension of Mickey Mouse. This is widly inaccurate. Instead, singlehandedly, it is engaged in replacing and extending many of those elements of the public realm which

Grauman's Chinese Theater in Los Angeles

have vanished in the featureless, private, floating world of Southern California, whose only edge is the ocean, and whose center is undiscoverable. Curiously, for a public place, Disneyland is not free. You buy your tickets at the gate. But then Versailles cost someone a great deal of money, too. Now, as then, you have to pay for the public life.

Disneyland is enormously important and successful just because it re-creates all the chances to respond to a *public* environment, which Los Angeles in particular does not have any longer. It allows play-acting, both to be watched and to be participated in. In as unlikely a place as could be conceived, just off the Santa Ana Freeway, a little over an hour from the Los Angeles City Hall, in an unchartable sea of suburbia, Disney created a place, indeed a whole public world, full of sequential occurrences. It has big and little drama, hier-archies of importance and excitement, with opportunities to respond at the speed of rocketing bobsleds (or rocketing rockets, for all that), or of horse-drawn streetcars. An American Main Street of about 1910 is the principal theme against which play fairy-tale fantasies, frontier adventure situations, jungles, and the world of tomorrow.

All this diversity, with unerring sensitivity, is keyed to the kind of partici-pation without embarrassment which apparently we crave. No raw edges spoil the picture at Disneyland. Everything is as immaculate as in the musical-comedy villages that Hollywood has provided for our viewing pleasure. Nice

117

Main Street in Disneyland

looking, handsomely costumed young people sweep away the gum wrappers almost before they fall to the spotless pavement. Everything works, the way it doesn't seem to any more in the world outside.

The skill demonstrated here in recalling with thrilling accuracy all sorts of other times and places is of course one which has been developing in Hollywood throughout this century. Disney's experts are breathtakingly precise when they recall the gingerbread of a turn-of-the-century Main Street or a side-wheeler Misissippi River steamboat, even while they remove the grime and mess, and reduce the scale to the tricky zone between delicacy and make-believe. Curiously, the Mickey Mouse/Snow White sort of thing, which is most memorably Disney's and which figures heavily in an area called Fantasyland, is not nearly so successful as the rest, since it perforce drops all the way over into the world of real make-believe.

Other occurrences stretch credulity but somehow avoid snapping it. The single most exciting experience in the place is that which involves taking a cable car in Fantasyland, soaring above its make-believe castles, then ducking through a large *papier maché* mountain called the Matterhorn, which turns out to be hollow and full of bobsleds darting about in astonishingly vertical directions. Whence one swings out above Tomorrowland. Nobody, of course, thinks that that mountain is the Matterhorn, or even a mountain, or that those bobsleds are loose upon its slopes — slopes standardly being on the outsides

The Matterhorn at Disneyland

of mountains. Yet the experience of passing that space is a real one, and an immensely exciting one, like looking at a Piranesi prison, or escalating in the London Underground.

Of course Disneyland, in spite of the skill and variety of its enchantments, does not offer the full range of public experience. The political experience, for instance, is not manifested there. Yet there is a variety of forms and activities great enough to ensure an excellent chance that the individual visitor will find something to identify with.

Methods of seeking "character" for buildings in northern California are mostly much less theatrical than in Southern California, and adhere more strictly to a single pattern, an outgrowth of the redwood Bay Region Style in the direction of the standard universal American motel, employing stucco walls, aluminum windows, wooden shakes, and casual, if not cavalier, attitudes toward form.

New monumental buildings in Northern California bear a firmer recollection of the residential Bay Region Style. They have achieved varying degrees of architectural and critical success. John Carl Warnecke's post office and book store adjoining the old campus at Stanford University uses its masonry walls and Mediterranean red tile roofs as a point of departure to make, with two large, steep overhanging roofs, a form almost strong enough to take its place beside the old campus. A finely detailed colonnade, roofed with hyperbolic

Stanford University Book Store, by John Carl Warnecke (above left)
Student Union at the University of California, Berkeley, by Vernon De Mars (above right)

paraboloids, tucks rather redundantly under the great tile overhang and fails to measure up to the rest. The care taken in forming its concrete members is, however, heartening assurance that the arts of construction have not yet died out.

At the University of California Student Union in Berkeley, Vernon De Mars has sought to induce an active public response by devising (in a manner that closely parallels Disney's) astonishing juxtapositions of fragments. Individually, they are often exquisitely designed, but they are left to fend for themselves in a hubbub meant to recall the chaos of the city. The forms, like Disney's, sometimes unabashedly recall another time or place: a steel trellis surmounting the major block of the building is said to owe allegiance to Bernard Maybeck's wooden ones of an earlier generation, though those generally bore vines. The spaces around the building are by way of appreciation of the *Piazza di San Marco*. The carefully developed street furnishings recall Scandinavia. But the scope offered for this collection of occurrences is by no means Disney's so that the chance to recreate the moods of the city is severely restricted. From the Student Union there is no aerial tramway direct to Tomorrowland, no Disney-land chance to create still another world.

Whatever is missing, however, this collector's approach to enlivening the public realm demonstrates real advantages over the single-mindedness of, say, the San Francisco City Hall or some of the soberer classroom blocks that stand

120

Hearst Mining Building, Berkeley, by John Galen Howard

about on the Berkeley campus. The simplicity and the anonymity of these high blocks, mostly tile-roofed, set on knolls in groves of oaks and giant eucalypti, are in the spirit of the Bay area, are praiseworthy, and have often been praised. But success eludes most of them, probably because they set out to recall the area's last two idioms, but seldom with enough conviction to rise above the perfunctory. The two local idioms they seek to recall were lively ones, and look lively still.

The first, a high-spirited explosion of Classical or other forms, which break apart to leave voids in astonishing places, so as to create lofty spaces and dark shadows, has left a major monument on the campus, the Hearst Mining Building of 1907. John Galen Howard was its architect. The second local idiom, in whose development William Wurster was the central figure, usually comes out best at small scale, since the carefully understated, spare, almost anonymous efficiency of a well-understood carpenter's constructional system is most clearly in evidence there. "No matter how much it costs," Catherine Bauer Wurster pointed out about her husband's work "it will never show." The new large buildings on the Berkeley campus of the University of California succeed because they share either in the exuberance of the first local idiom or in the naturalness of the second. When they fail, they fail from attempting continuity with the first local idiom (their great tile roofs lifted up and out of sight) or from seeking to cash in on the apparent casualness of the second local idiom, without noting that that is a casualness born of an intimate understanding of a constructional system and a way of life.

Not only the University, but all of California and the West, now face an architectural crisis different in many ways from the problems of the rest of the country. The Boston architects of the nineteenth-century railroad tycoon Leland Stanford had their own clear notions, social and architectural, of the nature of hierarchy, and they manifested them with great success in the old Stanford campus. But twentieth-century California has been egalitarian. As its population grows phenomenally, the people who comprise it, rich and poor, come from all sorts of places and owe no allegiance to any establishment of the sort that exercises at least some control of money and taste in areas less burgeoning.

While California was largely rural, this egalitarianism lent special delights to living there. In Southern California, from a combination of white-walled Spanish Colonial and the International Style, there developed, through Gill and Schindler and Neutra and *Arts and Architecture* magazine, and through the climate and the landscape, a way of building large numbers of private houses of a charm and comfort never before possible anywhere. This development was surpassed only in northern California. If the climate was a bit moodier there, the views of bays and forests were better; and there were architects, first of the generation of Bernard Maybeck, then of the generation

Street in Gilroy, California

of William Wurster, Gardner Dailey, and Hervey Parke Clark, who were willing and eminently able to make the most of the opportunities. They developed a domestic architecture not only esteemed by architects, but almost universally accepted and enjoyed by the people for whom it was made. This is the domestic architecture we can call the Bay Region Style.

California was once a golden never-never land with plenty of room, with open fields for the public realm, with magnificent scenery for a sharable image, and with Hollywood's grandiose offerings for a publicly sharable experience. Nothing then could have been more natural than this emphasis on provision for domestic life, nothing more understandable than the gradual atrophying of concern for a public realm that people go to and use. The public weal was being extensively considered in projects built hundreds of miles from Los Angeles and San Francisco to provide those cities with water and electric power. But the kind of monumentality that occurs when the Establishment requires buildings more important than other buildings in places of special importance never occurred. California during the first four decades of the twentieth century was being developed mostly at a domestic scale — and very well, too. It seemed quite proper that man's impact on the land should be of this cozy, egalitarian, and very pleasant sort.

This process, however, is continuing in the later twentieth century, and by now it brings worry. The domestic arrangements of the earlier decades are

123

being reproduced endlessly, no longer in the places that laid some claim to public attention — places like Bel Air, Berkeley, and Sausalito (for the view); San Francisco and San Diego (for the bay); Hollywood (for a very special activity); and Santa Barbara (for high mountains coming close to the sea). Instead they are being reproduced in the no-places in between — like Hayward, Daly City, Inglewood, Manchester, and other municipal fictions even less memorable. The character and the sense of special place that came for free to the first communities — from the oak trees around them and the yellow hills and the mountains and the sea — do not similarly serve the later comers. Indeed they do not serve anyone. The oak trees go, and the yellow hills vanish; the smaller mountains are flattened, and even portions of the sea are filled in, all to be covered in a most egalitarian way with endless houses. Even the movie studios are being covered up.

It occurs to some, while the gray domestic waves of this suburban sea fill in the valleys and the bays and erode the hills, that something should be done, and that that something should be urban and monumental. The Bay Region Style, for all its domestic triumphs, offers no architectural framework for making a special celebration. The characteristic Wurster reticence, which has served so well in helping to create the continuous domestic fabric of the Bay cities, is too deeply ingrained to allow that. In Southern California, a latter-day straightforwardness, born mostly of a habit of commercial expediency, mili-

The Rubin house in Albany, California, by George Homsey

tates against the architectural celebration of a particular place. But even more basic than the absence of an architectural idiom for making public centers is the absence of any Establishment ready to shoulder the responsibility for the public realm. So what, as we started out by asking, might we have instead for an architectural framework?

The first and best chance for these floating gray suburbs comes from our asking what the problems really are.

A few houses by a few architects, mostly under the immediate influence of Joseph Esherick, are especially concerned with the specific analysis of (and response to) the problems of site, its outlooks and climate, the client and his needs. This is not a revolution, really, away from the attitudes of the second Bay Region idiom; it embodies many of the same methods of direct response to the problem. But it seeks to clarify and extend these methods to cope with the aggravated situation.

Esherick's Cary House in Marin County, for instance, has a wooded view. But it does not rely on a wall of glass pointed in that direction; instead it has a wall with glass openings, each carefully placed to perform a specific function of admitting light, lighting a surface, or exposing a carefully selected portion of the view. The Rubin House in Albany, by George Homsey, though on a less dramatic site, reacts even more specifically to such local delights as the dappled light coming in between the eucalyptus leaves, and the usually hazy

125

The Graham house in Berkeley, California, by Richard Peters and Peter Dodge (above)
The Cary house in Mill Valley, California, by Joseph Esherick (opposite)

sun of the bay shore sliding through skylights and along white walls. The exterior of the Graham House, by Richard Peters and Peter Dodge, on a steep Berkeley hillside, also demonstrates forms that grow not from a generalized formal impulse but from a specific search for light, air, space, and outlooks. All this extends the simpler idiom of the earlier unformal Bay Region work toward what promises to be a much fuller vocabulary, generated, like its precursor, not by restrictive formal systems but by specific responses to specific problems. So far, these are restricted domestic problems. But there is no reason why the elusive problems of the public realm could not respond to sophisticated extensions of the same efforts.

For the opportunity to create a public realm, we must look to sources other than the Establishment, to people or institutions interested at once in public activity and in place. We depend, in part, on more Disneys, on more men willing to submerge their own Mickey Mouse visions in a broader prospect of greater public interest. They must be willing and able to focus their attention on a particular place. Disneyland, however arbitrary its location, is unique, even as Los Angeles is, and much of its power comes from that fact.

Until lately the largest single patron available to be pressed into service of the public realm has been the State Highway Department. Freeways have been one of the most serious generalizers of place in the state, ruthlessly and thoughtlessly severing some communities, congesting others, and obliterating

127

still others, marring, gouging, and wiping out whole landscapes. Yet, they loom large in the public eye as one of the biggest, strongest, most exciting, and most characteristic elements of the new California. If one had to name the center of Southern California, it would surely be the place not far from the Los Angeles City Hall where the area's major freeways wrap together in a graceful, strong, and much-photographed three-level interchange.

Much of the public excitement about San Francisco's small but dramatic skyline is a function of the capacity to see it, a capacity which is greatly enhanced by the bridges (themselves major California monuments) and by the freeways that lead to them. Indeed, in San Francisco, as in few places, the view which gives a sense of the whole city is one of the most valuable parts of the public realm. It is one of the parts that is most frequently attacked, and it must be most zealously defended. One of the public view's most effective defenders could be the freeway builders — though, admittedly, they have more often acted as saboteurs, as when they tried, and partly succeeded, in building a freeway wall between San Francisco and the bay.

The cities of California urgently need attention, before the characteristics that distinguish them at all are obliterated. There is no need, and no time, to wait for a not-yet-existent Establishment to build the traditional kind of monuments. Nor is there time for a disaster gripping enough to wake the public conscience to the vanishing places of the public realm we got for free. Most

Freeways in Los Angeles

effectively, we might first develop a vocabulary of forms responsive to the marvelously complex and varied functions of our society. Then we might start sorting out those things for which the public has to pay and from which we might derive the public life. These things would not be the city halls and equestrian statues of another place and time. They had better be something far better, and of far more public use.

They might, for instance, be freeways. Freeways are not for individual people (like living rooms are and like confused planners would have you believe the whole city ought to be). They are for the public use and are part of the public realm. If the fidgety structures beside them (and the deserts for parking — or for nothing — under them) do not make sense, it is surely because there has been too little understanding of the public realm, not too much. The freeways could be the real monuments of the future, the places set aside for special celebration by people able to experience space and light and motion and relationships to other people and things at a speed that only this century has allowed.

Here are structures big enough and strong enough, once they are regarded as a part of the city, to re-excite the public imagination about the city. This is no shame, to be covered by suburban bushes or quarantined behind cyclone fences. It is the marker for a place set in motion transforming itself to another place. The exciting prospects, not surprisingly, show up best at Disneyland.

129

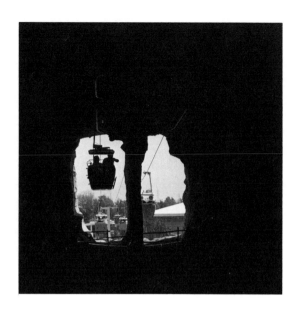

Inside the Matterhorn at Disneyland

There, on the inside of the Matterhorn from the aerial tramway over the bobsled run on the inside of the plastic mountain, is a vision of a place marked out for the public life, of a kind of rocketing monumentality, more dynamic, bigger and — who knows? — even more useful to people and to the public than any the world has yet seen.

C.M.

Discrimination in Housing Design

Discrimination in housing design — not between black and white, but between "front" and "back," "public" and "private," "ours" and "yours" — is a basic part of the process of contemporary housing design, and it may well be a basic part of its undoing. It is a technique taught in schools, practiced in architectural offices, and so well learned and so familiar that many designers never even question the fact that they are using it. It analyzes and dissects the problem at hand into discrete and (it is hoped) essential components.

Take, for instance, the colors on a planner's land-use map. They discriminate by consecrating whole areas of a city to some particular use. The governmental bureaucracies that regulate architectural design also make careful discriminations — like the one between circulation space in a building and habitable space, which assumes, we might guess, that it is not possible to circulate in a room or to inhabit a corridor.

Architects practice discrimination when they separate out all of the programmatic requirements for a building and assign some amount of square footage to each. Then, with the help of bubble diagrams or a "functional relationships matrix," they analyze and demonstrate how each part relates to all the other parts. They also make broad, general assumptions about "public" and "private" zones, and the zones needed for mechanical equipment and for vehicular and pedestrian circulation.

What results from all this analytical effort is a universe made up of discrete

Roehampton housing blocks, by the London County Council

parts. We learn to assume, first of all, that each of these parts can really be identified precisely, and, second, that each is only itself (green, say, on the planner's map) and not to some more or less subtle extent something else as well (red). These assumptions become surprisingly well ingrained, so that a lot of excitement can be generated among architects when they start talking about contrary notions like "mixed uses" in a building or a "mixed income" housing development. These kinds of buildings seem to deny the either/or relationship of parts (either green or red) and to substitute a less clearly schematic both/and. When asked, "What kind of building is that?" most of us find it easier to be able to say "offices for a multinational corporation" or "housing for the poor" — which is perhaps to say that most of us find it easier to cope with essential entities than with essential ambiguities.

Can designing by discrimination really be all that bad? Nobody, for sure, can deny that it makes perfectly good sense to understand a problem by trying to understand its parts. Accordingly, contemporary architectural practice has subjected just about every conceivable part of the design and construction process to discriminations. The process itself is seen as a collection of separate and simultaneous processes (architectural design, structural design, mechanical and electrical design, site planning, and so on), and its sequence is organized into a progression of separate stages (programming, schematic design, design development, and so forth).

Site plan of Roehampton (above left)
Private terraces in the Roehampton blocks (above right)

High-style twentieth-century architectural theory, moreover, has made a considerable point of trying to find essential and pure forms to express a building's function, and to separate them out from superficial and detractive details. An example of this propensity — and a beautiful one — can be seen in the housing blocks designed by the London County Council in Roehampton in the late 1950s. They are classic examples of Modern housing design, though their success may spring as much as anything else from the fact that Richmond Park, where they stand, is so evidently a nice place to live — in contrast to the sites of other twentieth-century classics, like St. Louis's infamous Pruitt-Igoe (or, for that matter, Marseilles's famous *Unité d'habitation*).

The design of the Roehampton housing is based on a host of careful discriminations. Two-story apartment units, whose separateness from each other is clearly indicated on the outside, gather together to form giant slabs which not only look different from the natural surroundings (because of their whiteness and their plain forms) but are actually separate from them (by virtue of being raised above the ground on columns). Notice how easy it is, even without identifying labels, to tell what is what on the site plan: buildings are clearly buildings, roads are roads, and footpaths footpaths — all beautifully distinct systems floating on a pleasant and undifferentiated greensward. Note, as well, how the presence of people and their wishes can pleasantly violate these discriminations — as in the case of the gardens which have migrated right up onto

133

A street in Little Venice in London (above)
Old and new buildings overlooking the canal in Little Venice (opposite top)
New housing in Little Venice, by Hubert Bennett (opposite center)
Site plan of the new housing (opposite bottom right)
Typical entry to the new housing (opposite bottom left)

the apartment terraces, the better to be tended by the inhabitants, and the worse to conform to the system.

Another example of discrimination in housing design, also in London and also by the London County Council, is their housing in Paddington — designed in an altogether Modern vocabulary, but carefully formed around an older neighborhood known as Little Venice. The site overlooks a small pond, made by the swelling of a barge canal and surrounded on three sides by handsome early- to mid-nineteenth-century houses. On the fourth side, replacing older, deteriorated buildings, is the Council housing. Its architects have tried to make the new buildings "fit" their older surroundings, and in many ways their success is very remarkable. The scale of the older facades, bays, and windows is carefully reflected in the new ones; so is their cream-painted stucco finish.

What is perhaps most remarkable about the Council housing, though, is the ways in which it is altogether different from the older houses around it — the ways it doesn't seem to fit at all. In the Council housing, every effort is made to make it clear just what is what, and what is whose. The front facade, for instance, is simply the aggregate expression of all the individual units, with nothing else added. The elderly residents all live in studio apartments on the ground floor, with entrances directly off a shared front terrace, itself separated from the adjacent sidewalk by an iron fence and a level change. Younger families all live in three-bedroom duplexes on the floors above, and these are entered

134

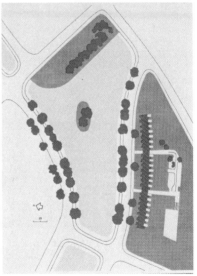

Older houses overlooking the canal in Little Venice

across bridges that lead from the sidewalk to unmemorable doorways and, beyond them, to shared stairways.

Notice, by contrast, how in the older houses nearby it is not at all clear what is what, or what is whose. One of them is actually a two-family house, though it is designed so as not quite to seem it. The design is a vivid example of the use of double scale. The front porch, the columns, the pilasters, the balustrade, and the little central attic story are all elements in a system whose largest part is the entire facade. But, on the other hand, the actual front doors, the first- and second-story windows, and the pair of attic windows set in a common frame form another, different system that begins to tell of the house's duplicity. Similarly, but more extensively, another house overlooking the canal groups together three separate houses with its large cornice and engaged Corinthian columns and pilasters. Though this building is a collection of individual dwelling units, it is — in the splendid tradition of grander Georgian terrace houses — made to seem one great house. It is, moreover, the one great house whose presence is noted along the street — and the dwellers in each of its parts can, if they wish, share in its publicity.

For better or for worse, these older houses are examples of the "inclusive" architecture we have described earlier in this book (pages 6, 51-60). Are they houses, or are they housing? Who lives where? What parts belong to whom? These buildings include many alternatives for what they might be — and they

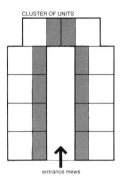

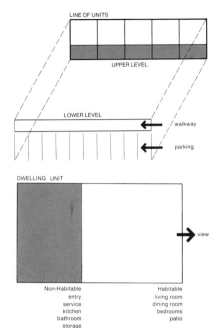

LINE OF UNITS

UPPER LEVEL

LOWER LEVEL

walkway

parking

CLUSTER OF UNITS

entrance mews

DWELLING UNIT

view

Non-Habitable	Habitable
entry	living room
service	dining room
kitchen	bedrooms
bathroom	patio
storage	
stair	

Diagrams for the Whitney Road Residential Development in Perrinton, New York, by
Gwathmey Siegel Architects

also include us, enticing us into asking these very questions.

The Council housing, on the other hand, is an example of "exclusive" architecture. It is quite clear what it is, and what its component parts are. It speaks its piece forthrightly, and the statement is one that is based on discriminations.

Similarly discriminatory is the design for a low-rise, low-density housing development in Perrington, New York. It was designed in the early 1970s by New York City architects Charles Gwathmey and Robert Siegel, and they have published a series of diagrams that describe how they went about their work. These diagrams reveal a seemingly logical process. First, space in the individual apartment units is divided into "habitable" and "non-habitable" zones. The units are then clustered in one of two ways, with the non-habitable areas always facing the "public" zones and the habitable areas facing the "views." Next, these clusters are gathered into larger groups, and, with the imposition of the vehicular circulation diagram, the site plan finally emerges.

Gwathmey and Siegel's diagrams seem conspicuously reasonable. They embody a set of analytical assumptions that, once made, seem to march inexorably toward an architectural solution. For this reason (and because so many architects have been taught to design in just this way) these diagrams provide an instructive example of the way an overly exclusive analysis can not only falsify the problem at times, but can also seem so incisive and so compelling

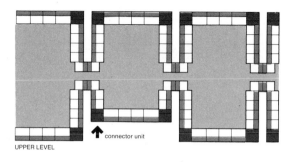

UPPER LEVEL

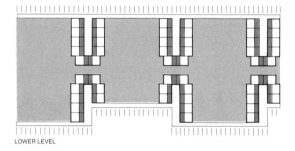

LOWER LEVEL

Gwathmey Siegel diagrams

that it gets mistaken for a solution. The diagnosis, that is, can beguilingly wind up as the cure.

At the outset, the architects' distinctions between habitable and non-habitable spaces in each dwelling unit seem perfectly sensible, and they recall other more or less similar discriminations — like Louis I. Kahn's[1] "served" and "servant" spaces, or Robert Venturi's[2] "unspecific" and "specific" spaces and, for that matter, the distinction that Charles Moore, Donlyn Lyndon, and I[3] have made between "rooms" and "machine domains". Some people, however, might wonder about Gwathmey and Siegel's terminology: should not a kitchen or a stairway be "habitable," or at least not uninhabitable, just like a living room?

In any case, the point is this: a distinction is being made between two kinds of interior spaces. It may be a very good one, but, once made, it establishes a pattern for further, parallel distinctions that may turn out to be much less appropriate, since they may turn out to be responding more to the abstract system than to the real dimensions of the problem at hand. Thus the distinction here between habitable and non-habitable spaces seems to require that all of the so-called habitable spaces face the entrance side of the dwelling units. Parking naturally goes on this side, and so do the roads for the cars to arrive on. This becomes a kind of "public" side. By contrast, the view goes on the other side, where it can be enjoyed from the habitable spaces; this becomes a kind of "private" side.

138

entrance mews

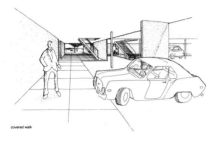

covered walk

Sketches for the Whitney Road Residential Development

So the result of this chain of discriminations — subtle, and certainly un-intentional — is that there can get to be a "good" side and a "bad" side. The bad side is the result of separating out elements in the design that are less attrac-tive and more problematical (like the accomodation of parked cars) or poten-tially dangerous (like the paths the cars move on) and lumping them together, away from the other, nicer things. This process, incidentally, which is here described purely in terms of architectural design, is startingly similar to what happens in cases of social discrimination, where the people who are discri-minated against all end up together in a ghetto, with the seemingly irresistible power to gather all of the physical and economic and social ills of the society around them. And so it is well worth asking whether or not too ruthless a dis-crimination by the architect between public and private, for instance, may not unintentionally but inevitably lead to disastrous discriminations between "yours" and "ours," "dangerous" and "safe," or "bad" and "good."

The problem is to include people and their caring in all the parts. A sure measure of how successful certain housing is is how well people like it, and how well they like it is surely reflected in how much their care for it shows. The housing itself may provide a vehicle for caring, and it may express it directly, as in the meticulous gingerbread details in the little houses at Oak Bluffs on Martha's Vineyard in Massachusetts. Or the caring may be expressed by the inhabitants in contradiction of the architectural format, as we have seen it do

Houses in Oak Bluffs on Martha's Vineyard

at Roehampton, where the residents have made gardens on the terraces of their apartments, contrary to the design "concept" which separates the natural (Richmond Park) from the man-made (the concrete slabs).

By the same token, the absence of signs of caring may well signal bad housing, no matter where it occurs. People's sense that there is nothing in the general environment worth caring about, or that their concern will not make any difference, or that it will be swamped — all this may very well be a *cause*, not just a result, of bad places to live in. And *its* effect may not be simply the standard ones that most of us have heard about but probably not actually had to deal with: violent crime in city streets laden with garbage. Its effect may finally extend to wide suburban streets inhabited mostly by fat cars, and to houses whose blank faces and open garages say that the caring is out back by the barbecue and the swimming pool.

The solution to these problems — insofar as architecture by itself has any power to solve broad social problems — is bound to be in a kind of residential environment that involves people actively, that at least does not discourage care in any of its parts, and that, with any luck, invites it in them all.

What will that entail? For one thing, it may entail avoiding foolish consistency, however appealing consistency may be. Consider, for instance, the case of the schematic design for a house that has public space in front, private space out back, the car in the carport, the furnace in the furnace room, and

A suburban street in Charlotte, North Carolina

kitchen, baths, bedrooms, and living room all neatly consigned to their proper places. It makes a logical system — an abstract representation lying on the architect's drawing board. But its problem may be this: for all its diagrammatic clarity it may be really at odds with a totally different kind of consistency — that of the human sensibility, which presumably does not change as it moves from the garage (which may be cold and damp and cluttered) or from the public space (which may be dangerous) to inside the house to the kitchen (perhaps designed around the machines more than for the owner's comfort) or to the living room (which may be completely splendid). In cases like this, a consistency of form will have been substituted for a continuity of experience.

Earlier in this book we have looked at buildings — St. Thomas Church, the Santa Barbara County Courthouse, the Carpenter Center, the Cannery, and a house by the Cannery's architect — which eschew formal consistencies, the private little drawing-board victories, in favor of the perceptions of the people who must behold them. Many readers will note that many of these buildings look un-Modern and traditional. We find no cause for alarm in that, for, in being traditional, architecture can clothe the specialness of single buildings in the partial likenesses of other things, outward through culture and backward in time. Thus it can become a paradigm of the world, the reflection of the traditional struggle to reconcile personal individuality with a social whole — like the nineteenth-century houses in Little Venice, which gradually and

A suburban street in Charlotte, North Carolina

---

ambiguously gird their individual selves together to make something that is more than themselves. The message of buildings like this to architects should be straight-forward and clear: Invite involvement. Invite care.

G.A.

Southernness: A regional dimension

If John F. Kennedy did indeed call Washington, D.C., a city of southern efficiency and northern charm, it was a statement characterized less by its deadly
accuracy and double-edged sharpness than by the startling lack of ambiguity
which went with it. The American north is prized for its efficiency and the
opulence of its progress. The American south is seen to lack those qualities
and to rely instead on more leisurely (and more charming) ways. There is, of
course, across the world a continuing distinction between the north (of Italy,
say), industrial and progressive, and the south, rural and poor. Even when big
cities are found in the south, the differences still are often noted. I have lately
heard a careful distinction between the north of Louisiana, sharp and dour,
and the south around New Orleans, more leisured and gracious — and urbane.

It is, in fact, a kind of scaled-down urbanity which seems to me, a north-
erner, the most powerful southern image. Because of my affection for that
quality and that part of the country, I am taking the liberty of writing about
the South's contribution to American architecture. The only parallel discussion
I can remember was Lewis Mumford's[1] in 1941. He had looked at the south
mostly through two great architects, Thomas Jefferson (who came, as we all
know, from Virginia) and Henry Hobson Richardson (who came from
Louisiana, but did his work from Boston). I, on the other hand, think it is
worthwhile to start from a collection of buildings and towns in the South which
have maintained their hold on me, and to try to discern what they have in
common.

143

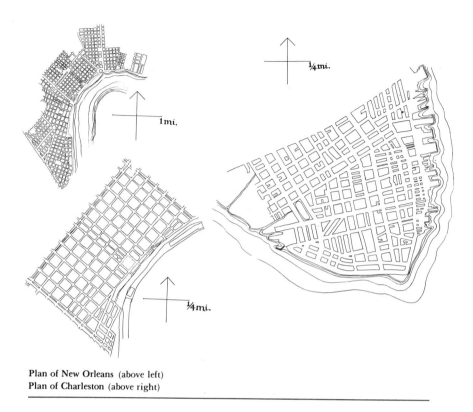

Plan of New Orleans (above left)
Plan of Charleston (above right)

One thing my assembled places do not share is local authorship. The architects came from England and France, and later from Rhode Island and New York, as well as from Charlottesville and Charleston. Many only visited the South. And many, of course, were not professional architects at all, but engineers (like L'Enfant), gentlemen colonizers (like Oglethorpe), or, especially, a Renaissance man, Thomas Jefferson.

The South, as it is generally taken (from the Mason-Dixon line to the Gulf of Mexico, and from the Atlantic to Texas) has a variety of climates, from the sharp seasonal differences of the Blue Ridge mountains and the Smokies to the almost tropical Gulf Coast. But almost all of the South has long hot summers, which induce the tempo some of us connect with charm. (Others link it with indolence and poverty.) All of the area, too (except for a corner north of Washington) shares a past which includes the institution of black slavery, secession from the Union, a bloody and debilitating war, and a slow and painful recovery. The sense of local autonomy which prompted the secession is now generally well regarded across the country (but black slavery, of course, is not; if you ask at Mount Vernon where the slaves' quarters are, you will be shown the "dependencies"). So the climate and the institutional inheritance may provide direction in our search for architectural southernness, even if the backgrounds of the architects do not.

It is the collection itself that will provide most of the clues. It includes

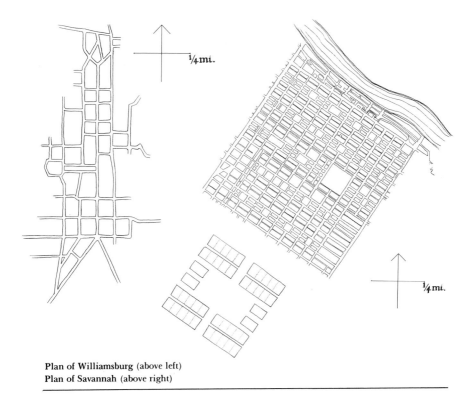

Plan of Williamsburg (above left)
Plan of Savannah (above right)

places especially memorable. It leaves out gardens, which deserve a separate study, and humble rural dwellings, which do too. It also leaves out examples from the present century, at least partly because buildings built during the heyday of the energy blowout have been air conditioned by refrigeration, so they have lost some of their reason for specialness, and have come closely to resemble buildings elsewhere. If I could have pinpointed that magic moment in the 1930s when Miami Beach became the first place in the world to resemble, albeit in miniature, Le Corbusier's *Ville Radieuse*, I should have done that as well.

The places I remembered and chose are, alphabetically:

Biltmore House, near Asheville, North Carolina, designed for George Washington Vanderbilt in 1890 by Richard Morris Hunt of New York.

Bremo plantation, in Virginia, designed by its owner, General John Hartwell Cocke after 1817, with strong Jeffersonian influence.

Charleston, the city, developed after 1730, including especially the following: St. Michael's Church, built 1752-61, and designed by a Mr. Samuel Cardy, an Irishman, or perhaps by James Gibson of South Carolina, or possibly even by the English architect James Gibbs; and the Nathaniel Russell house, built by 1811, and designed by Russell Warren of Rhode Island.

Monticello, near Charlottèsville, Virginia, designed in several stages between 1770 and 1808 by its owner Thomas Jefferson, a Virginian with books

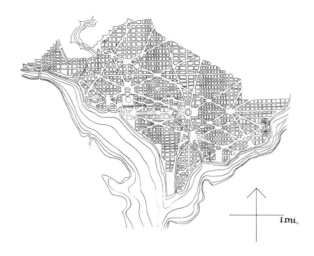

1 mi.

Plan of Washington

from Italy and England and strong memories of France.

Mount Vernon, south of Alexandria, Virginia, more casually put together and expanded in the eighteenth century by its owner, General George Washington.

Another city in a coastal swamp, *New Orleans*, founded in 1718 and expanded thereafter under French, Spanish and American regimes.

The city of *Savannah*, as it was laid out in 1733 according to a plan by James Oglethorpe, an aristocratic English entrepreneur, perhaps after a scheme described in Venice in 1567 by Pietro di Giacomo Cataneo.[2]

Stratford Hall, in Westmoreland County, Virginia, designed for the Lee family by a strong but unknown hand in about 1725.

The *University of Virginia*, the work of Thomas Jefferson, accomplished in the years after 1810.

The city of *Washington*, an overlay of Baroque radial patterns, developed by Major Pierre L'Enfant of France, and a Classical grid, proposed by Thomas Jefferson.

And finally, *Williamsburg*, the capital of Virginia until the end of the eighteenth century, put together by its English governors.

These places, both cities and buildings, with the eventual exception of Washington, D.C., are mostly quite small, mostly possessed of a high degree of geometric order, and must have been through most of their existence swarm-

146

Stratford Hall in Virginia

ing with inhabitants. Therein lies their special quality, and the essential para-
dox of this collection. The heavily populated industrial cities of this country
have been mostly in the North (where attitudes, as Vincent Scully[3] has pointed
out, were non- or even anti-urban, and the life of the imagination was focused
on the limitless frontier). The much more rural South, at once small-scaled and
monumental, hyped up by the ferocity of its summers, achieved a pitch of
public inhabitation only describable as urban, and urbane.

Even the great houses in this collection must once have been extraordinarily different from the hushed delicacy of their twentieth-century selves.
The guides at Stratford Hall, as they show off the bedrooms (with one bed each),
describe a variety of eighteenth-century Lees and their attendants and guests,
whose simultaneous tenancy must have caused Stratford Hall to approach the
residential density of Hong Kong. Their togetherness, on a sultry summer
afternoon, must have been an altogether different phenomenon from the late-
twentieth-century solution to the heat (far more effective and deadly) which
organizes the population into individual refrigerators for the long summer
months.

Whole cities, too — especially coastal ones like Charleston and New
Orleans — were pressed by the swampy ground into quite restricted compass,
then opened up internally to catch any summer breeze. They must have been
models of pell-mell urban vivacity, with life in the streets at an almost Venetian

Jackson Square in New Orleans

intensity. In the Vieux Carré, the original part of New Orleans, the density of urban life was intensified in the early nineteenth century as the narrow streets were lined with buildings whose grilled balconies overhung the sidewalks. In such a fine-grained urban scene, acts of geometric formality, even gentle ones, can exert enormous power. The Baroness Pontalba's twin apartment blocks, altogether simple, with just three generous stories and continous balconies along the upper floors, grant in their symmetry a real sense of the center of things (an urban sense) to Jackson Square, which they flank. The rather unprepossessingly spiky cathedral, in the center of the composition, flanked by government buildings of simple elegance (the Cabildo and the Presbytère), is thrust into a position of much-increased importance by the Pontalba apartments along the square's sides. For contrast, one might consider a typical twentieth-century new town, and wonder where in, say, Columbia, Maryland, one might place two three-story apartment blocks to have any effect on the urban scene at all.

The urban fabric of Charleston, South Carolina, which also had eighteenth-century beginnings is, as the plan suggests, somewhat less formal. It incorporates, however, a number of house types (at least one of them invented for this very site) which sought quite specifically to improve the quality of comfort along this steamy coast and, in doing that, established the pattern for an altogether memorable city. The special house form, the Charleston "single"

148

A house in Charleston (above left)
The Nathaniel Russell house in Charleston (above right)

house, occurs often. In an incident of urban cooperation now regulated out of existence, the system places long houses one room wide at right angles to the street, with a two- or three-story piazza, off which all the rooms open and which runs along the narrow garden. The windows of the house next door pick up air from this same garden, but no valuable space is wasted on a set-back. All of the lot is rendered habitable, all the rooms have natural through-ventilation and adjacent space on a shaded piazza, and every house has a garden. Entrance is generally right off the street, often highly elaborated to celebrate the passage from the public sidewalk outdoors to the private realm (still outdoors) which begins just inside the door.

Smaller Charleston houses relegate the garden to the rear and adjoin their neighbors in rows along the street. Grander houses expand in a format which allows generous vertical spaces inside, as in the Nathaniel Russell house, where a chimney of air is induced, and the stage is set for gracious sweeping movements by ladies in wide-flowing finery. All these building types are set within the limits (disciplined by the climate and the scarcity of land) of a dense urban fabric which allows nuances — like the forward thrust of the porch and spire of St. Michael's Church — to have powerful visual consequences, assuring the importance of St. Michael's.

By all odds, however, the most highly developed urban geometry in the South (or the country) is that of Savannah, Georgia, which was planned

St. Michael's Church in Charleston

around an expandable series of squares by James Oglethorpe, the English gentleman who founded the place on a bluff above the Savannah River. The most remarkable quality about the plan is the great variety of building sites it provides within such an apparently simple framework, and the alternate traffic patterns it allows. At each square are four monumental building sites, visible across the width of the square, each public on three sides. Along the long sides of each square, more modest building plots share their amenity with the neighboring buildings, which slip off in an unbroken row down the block, not actually facing the square but not really cut off from it either. The most memorable streets, meanwhile (those perpendicular to the river), have been spared from heavy traffic by the squares themselves, which provide monuments on axis which require slow-speed circumnavigation each time. Thus major traffic is relegated to the alternate straight streets which harbor commerce, leaving pockets of residential peace around almost all the squares. Streets parallel to the river slip alongside the squares uninterrupted, landward of the pair of commercial streets closest to the river. The houses, which are generally row houses in this dense fabric, usually have their main rooms raised one floor off the street for improved circulation of air under the elegantly high ceilings.

The Williamsburg, Virginia, that we see today, restored to a cinematic purity and elegance, was once a much more casual collection of buildings than its counterparts farther south, and it was also very small. But even the short

Duke of Gloucester Street in Williamsburg

and very wide main street, named for the Duke of Gloucester, has a collegiate building (perhaps after designs by Christopher Wren) on axis at one end, and a capitol at the other. It passes a long Baroque allée which leads to a Governor's Palace, as well as bisecting a courthouse square. The buildings of the town, not subject to the densifying pressures of Charleston, New Orleans, or Savannah, are mostly free-standing in gardens. But along Duke of Gloucester Street they almost touch, and face directly on the sidewalk. There is in the shops on the ground floors of these houses a still-strong hint of the mixed uses which must have contributed to the bustle of life in this small but important city.

Thomas Jefferson, who went to school there, thought that Williamsburg was an architectural disaster area and thought it mandatory, in the new republic he was helping to establish, that architecture and planning function in a much more sophisticated and important way than it had in the fairly casual aggregation of tiny monumental buildings in Williamsburg. So although he had in mind a grid plan for the new national capital, philosophically more perfect as well as more convenient, he could not have been altogether displeased with Major L'Enfant's baroque allées, especially since they were laid out with extraordinary sensitivity to the natural features of the site — from the hills (like Capitol Hill) to the waterways (which would have put the Washington monument almost on the shore, and allowed a splendid cascade down the hill west

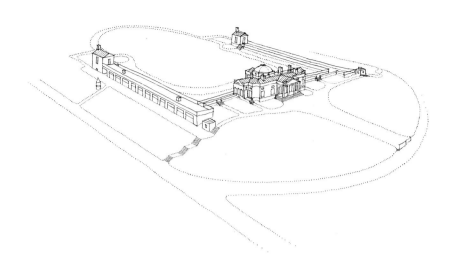

152

Bremo, in Virginia (above)
Monticello, in Virginia (opposite top)
Mount Vernon, in Virginia (opposite bottom)

of the Capitol) even to the irregular landward boundary at the Piedmont (now Florida Avenue).

If these southern cities were like houses, sensitive to their sites, dense, formally coherent, and full of a shared life, an even more evident source of southern urbanity is the houses that are like cities. These are jammed with a complexity of people but ordered with architectural devices establishing a formal dignity that makes them achieved places, not gateways to somewhere else in the accepted way of much of the rest of the country. Even Mount Vernon (which has the most disorderly plan of the great houses in this collection) makes a single grand public gesture with its portico toward the Potomac (the chief entrance, when the house was new). But on the other side its flanking galleries quite gently embrace a whole village of one-story "dependencies."

Thomas Jefferson spent the happiest hours of a long lifetime making his house at Monticello into a city, fitting it onto and into its mountaintop, crowning the hill with a monumental house-pavilion memorable enough — and symbolic enough — for the country he was helping to form, so that it seems appropriate that its image graces one of our country's coins. Here the theme "house" is stated in the one-room building which Jefferson built first, and to which he brought his bride. He then elaborated the theme through the complex workings of a vast establishment, mostly tucked into the hill and subordinated to it in a highly organized set of galleries. The whole was finally surmounted

Pavilion IX at the University of Virginia, by Thomas Jefferson (above)
Plan of the University of Virginia (opposite top)
The Rotunda, University of Virginia (opposite bottom)

by the monumental pavilion, capitol, place of welcome, and sign.

Jefferson's influence on Bremo, in Virginia, must have contributed to making it, on an only slightly more modest scale, into the same kind of ordered miniature urban complex as Monticello itself, a cut less ambitious and a cut more coherent.

But the quintessential house-city of them all is Thomas Jefferson's part of the University of Virginia. It is clearer, I think, than any other set of buildings on this continent, with qualities of invention and reflection and passion for architecture and the life lived in it. It is a plan for a university education made manifest in buildings on a site, with a place for reading and assembly at its head and professors' houses flanked by places for students' residence, with a chance to embody in the houses everything from the most solid Palladian architectural models to the latest from Ledoux, the whole democratized, socialized and linked by a continuing colonnade. It is the world of the mind in microcosm, and a splendid place to sit and work or talk or entertain friends.

One last special quality of the South began to show up late in the last century: its exoticism. Its Transylvanian sense of separateness from a rapidly-changing world, especially evident after the Civil War, prompted northern architects not just to import exotic styles (which they would have done anywhere) but to pursue them all the way to fairyland, to create a complete exotic world. It was French, in the Smoky Mountains, and Spanish (with more evident

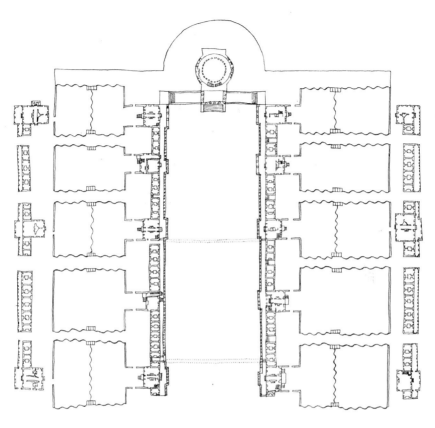

Biltmore House near Ashville, North Carolina, by Richard Morris Hunt

local reason) in St. Augustine, Florida, or, somehow, Moorish in Tampa. Then Addison Mizner pursued, in the early years of this century, the Spanish style on the east coast of Florida.

There is nothing newer in this collection, not because nothing has been built, but because the advent of air conditioning by refrigeration has hastened the loss of that special set of challenges of climate and site that provided the lively, urbane, and withal, charming cities and buildings in this collection.

C.M.

Modesty: If it's not the end, it's certainly the beginning

Perhaps one of the most useful contributions that the idea of orthodox Modern architecture has made to our environment during the past few decades is the one which it has made by becoming an object of derision among some architects and among many members of the general public. By seeming to represent everything that has been built, it has the power to suggest what might have been built instead, and thus it has become the unwitting sponsor of a quite extensive search for alternative ways to build our cities and towns.

The number of different directions in which people are searching is remarkable, and it is also reassuring. From the vantage point of the mid-1970s, Modern architecture has acquired some very general and very simple attributes in the popular imagination. It seems awesome and therefore powerful, austere and therefore unfriendly, abstract and therefore inhuman, unyielding and therefore authoritarian. It is important to note that all of these adjectives have meanings far beyond what is required simply to describe the physical qualities of a building, since this fact confirms the belief that architecture does indeed have a host of dimensions beyond the familiar three, and that the kind of architecture we choose to build can affect people's imaginations as well as their bodies, their dreams as well as their physical needs.

One of the current problems seems to be that, in a world which is evidently pluralistic and which serves up a myriad of different situations and experiences, standard Modern architecture always seems to come out the same. Efforts to

The Senior Services Center of the Pilot Center in Cincinnati, by Woollen Associates (above)
A street in Cincinnati's Over-the-Rhine district, with the Pilot Center on the left (opposite)

solve this problem have concentrated on two broad fronts. One of them is purely visual and formal, and it involves making buildings that are more responsive to the places where they are built. The other effort is more complex, since it involves paying more subtle attention to the whole range of economic, social, and political currents that define what a building really should be.

Two projects that are examples of both these trends are by the Indianapolis architectural firm of Woollen Associates, and they are worth looking at for the solutions they propose and the questions they raise. The first is the Pilot Center in Cincinnati's Over-the-Rhine district. It is a complex of four separate recreational and social-service facilities that occupy what was originally two city blocks, weaving their way in among older neighborhood buildings and, on the street, filling in the gaps left by previous demolitions.

Over-the-Rhine is a neighborhood that is about 45 percent black, 45 per cent Appalachian white, and 10 per cent of German extraction. It has been suffering from many of the familiar, self-compounding ills of older urban neighborhoods — deterioration of housing, loss of population, and low average incomes (about $4500 a year) among those who remain. Thus what was once a well-knit social (and architectural) fabric had begun to unravel.

But planners and residents who hoped for a brighter future for Over-the-Rhine did not place their hopes on the çi-devant panacea of wholesale urban renewal. Instead, they opted for a more meticulous process of retaining whatever

Aerial view of the Pilot Center and its neighborhood (above)
Entrance to the recreation building in the Pilot Center (opposite)

old buildings were sound, and therefore retaining the image and character of the district. Initially, only one part of it — dubbed the Target Area — was singled out for study by planners, and at its heart was the 1850 Findlay Market, an open-air meat and produce center diagonally across from the A & P store shown in the photograph above. In the planners' view, Findlay Market had an importance to the Target Area analogous to the importance of a shopping center in a contemporary suburb. Most of the key new buildings, therefore, would be built close by it.

So the Pilot Center is only one cog in the Target Area wheel. In order to maximize contact with local residents, Woollen Associates planned it from a branch office in a store near the site. The largest of the four buildings in the center is the recreational building, seen at the top of the photograph above and on the right. A community service building is beside it, and across the interior courtyard are a Senior Citizen Center and a school and day-care building. The spire in the photograph on the right is the surviving remnant of an 1840 Roman Catholic church, demolished to make way for the new recreational building — a loss to the cause of historic preservation, and also to the architects, who argued for its retention.

Evans Woollen describes his firm's work as "situational" architecture — an architecture that bends every effort to be particular to the place where it is built. In the case of their New Harmony Inn, the place is a midwestern town

160

Entry House of the New Harmony Inn, by Woollen Associates (above)
A street in New Harmony, Indiana, with the New Harmony Inn beyond (opposite)

of some 900 people, founded in 1814 by a communal sect of German Lutherans who called themselves Rappites. Recently, New Harmony has become the subject of a major development program designed to turn it into an important center for tourism and educational programs. The new 45-room inn is a major part of this refurbishing.

Woollen Associates' first design for it, done in the late 1960s, was strongly neo-Corbusian. Though it was in the end not built because the land could not be acquired, it elicited strong reactions. "It had a lot of amenities," Woollen says, "but nothing to do with New Harmony; people thought something would be lost if it were built." The town itself has several strong and readily identifiable qualities. The older buildings are no more than three stories high, and the important ones are made of brick, while the less important ones are of wood. None of them, moreover, seem quite as memorable as the overall format of the town, which is characterized by streets lined with beautiful trees.

The new inn is designed to reinforce the existing context. "By virtue of its having been off the beaten track, there is a built-in respect for context in New Harmony," Woollen says, "People in the 1870s went right on building like they had in the 1840s; their own world was bigger and more real than the world outside. It was as though a bell jar had been put over the town — and with the new inn we didn't want to let too much air in."

Thus the design for it stands in contrast to the design for the Pilot Center

Original Rappite dormitory in New Harmony (above left)
Aerial view of the inn, with Philip Johnson's "roofless church" at the lower left (above right)
New Harmony Inn, with Entry House on the right (opposite)

in Cincinnati. It also stands in contrast to Philip Johnson's more aggressive, and famous, "roofless church," which is virtually next door, and which can be seen in the lower left-hand corner of the aerial photograph above. Recent reports from New Harmony, however, indicate that the deterioration of the church's ten-foot wall, and its consequent reduction in height by about a half, have resulted in a happier scale relationship between it and the rest of the town.

The New Harmony Inn consists of two separate buildings: the smaller one, and the one nearest the street, is the entry house, containing a lobby and a large lounge, suitable for lectures and small concerts. The larger building — or "dormitory," in allegiance to the lore of New Harmony — is organized not along long corridors, but according to an entry system, with rooms opening directly onto one of three stairways.

Woollen Associates' design for the New Harmony Inn seems in every way "situational" — just like their design for the Pilot Center. Both buildings are in almost every way modest, responding sensitively to the places where they are built. But that raises a very important question: in being so modest, so particular to their places, are they being at all particular to themselves (presuming, as we usually do, that buildings are each meant to be in some way quite special)? Certainly no one could argue very strongly with the basic good sense of Woollen Associates' approach in these two cases. Whether or not the "situational" approach satisfies everyone's expectations of what archi-

164

tecture should always be, it seems worth pointing out that it is certainly where it might well begin.

G.A.

Schindler and Richardson

Some dimensions are a function of the architect himself, his visions and his limits. Consider Rudolph Schindler and H. H. Richardson, as discussed in two recent books about them.

David Gebhard's[1] book about Rudolph Schindler was, for me, the most moving story of an architect that I have read since I was astonished at an early age by Frank Lloyd Wright's autobiography. Being moved, of course, can include a lot more than transport on the wings of the dove, and it is this book's special quality that the bittersweet victories (or were they defeats?) of a fine, flawed career are brought so close and made so tense that for paragraphs at a time I imagined I was Schindler or he I.

It tells the story of a young man born in Vienna and trained there, who continued his training after 1914 in Chicago and then with Frank Lloyd Wright, on whose business he went to Los Angeles in 1920. From then until he died in 1953, Schindler's story was part of the exotic development of Southern California, bizarre then but the forerunner, as it turned out, for much of the rest of the world. It is this part of the story that Gebhard tells with special insight from which he extracts the full poignancy of the recent past in a sunny place now engulfed as surely as the lost Atlantis, buried under itself, submerged in people and their wholesale constructions and their noxious fumes.

Schindler's renown in Southern California was engulfed, even as he practiced, by the far more slickly-packaged reputation of his Viennese contempor-

Falk Apartments in Los Angeles, by Rudolph Schindler

ary, Richard Neutra, and by his own failure ever to get any really substantial commissions. It is one of the sympathetic wonders of Gebhard's work that he perceives Schindler's ideas, even the little ideas, even when they were aborted, and makes clear how these saved Schindler from the despair that so small a set of opportunities might have induced.

There are, happily, an impressive number of books around today about architects too soon forgotten, especially the contemporaries of Richardson and Wright. It turns out that many of them did large, handsome, and inspiring buildings. Why then bother with Schindler, whose body of work was small and inexpensive and (to my eyes) wildly erratic in quality? The answer, for me, was voiced in a radio interview I lately heard, in which a famous actor was praising a young actress with whom he had worked, and whom he had much admired. He searched for a word to describe her, and came up with *vulnerable* — that is to say, open to all kinds of things (nobody is open to everything) in the world around. Rudolph Schindler seems to have been vulnerable, too, and I like to think I am. His vulnerability caused him pain, and lost him work, and created some terrible looking buildings as well as some of lasting power. In this respect Schindler stands not only for himself but for a great many other vulnerable architects as well — most of them summarily dismissed by historians as "derivative."

Bona fide vulnerability, as I see it, involves caring about the specific things

Waverly house in Los Angeles, by Rudolph Schindler

you find, and find out about, so much that you will change your position to accommodate them. Invulnerable architects see and learn things too, but they have a position, or a sense of mission, early arrived at, to which the learned and seen things contribute, without the power to change it. Vulnerable and invulnerable is not good and bad. Moshe Safdie's *Beyond Habitat*[2] is the proud story of an invulnerable who has seen and known and felt a great deal, to the greater glory of his steady vision. Maybe there could be an historical game: I like to think that Bernini was invulnerable, and that Borromini was vulnerable. Some architects perhaps are vulnerable to a point, and then fix their positions. I am willing to believe that Louis I. Kahn's AFL-CIO Medical Center in Philadelphia was the work of a vulnerable, his Exeter Library of an invulnerable (this excuses me for preferring the former); Walter Gropius was the thoughtful arch-invulnerable, the International Style the temple of invulnerability.

I prefer distinctions like this that have good and bad on both hands. The one David Gebhard uses, to some of the same ends, is between high art and low art, and he sees Schindler's translations from the one to the other, either way, as contributing to his strength. I do not really dispute the existence of the chasm between high art and low, or the tense drama of the leap over it. But I do think the distinction is more useful to the gallery world of painting and sculpture (where some things deemed to be high art acquire very special attributes and price tags) than to architecture (where buildings submitted for our periodic

169

H. H. Richardson in the parlor-library of his house in Brookline, Massachusetts, about 1880

ritual premiation generally have much in common with and only some distinction from the "folk" work of our rich contractor friends). Schindler's work is common but very special in ways which make it tense and bittersweet, and more than a little unnerving.

Reading the book, I kept being reminded of my first trip to Japan, when I was aspiring to be a Bay Region architect. I had been to Europe, and had been transported by the presence of Chartres and the Parthenon and the Alhambra and Batalha; but I wasn't threatened by them. They were made of beautiful alien stuff. Now here in Japan were people who had taken boards — just what I used, though theirs appeared to be of better quality — and had made with them things more wonderful than I had ever dreamed of. That was threatening. And, of course, it was moving too.

Rudolph Schindler did things I try to do, and did some of them thrillingly well, and was never a success really, but kept responding all the while. That's what I'm moved by.

The catalogue by James F. O'Gorman[3] of selected drawings from a recent Henry Hobson Richardson exhibition, on the other hand, is as revealing a document about the modern practice of architecture as I have ever seen. It commands one's attention, to begin with, because some of the drawings are so simply, hauntingly beautiful, and it rivets one's attention for its continuing revelation of the power of economy.

Facade of Trinity Church in Boston, by H. H. Richardson

Economy of effort is not a quality I had ever thought to associate with such an apparent biterminal candle-burner as H. H. Richardson. Mrs. Schuyler van Rensselaer's[4] biography concentrates on his expansive charm; Henry-Russell Hitchcock's[5] concentrates on establishing him as a Modern architect (which seems to be a dubious proposition to begin with, and especially worrisome when so many of the tenets of Modern architecture are fading, and Richardson's reputation remains secure). But this catalogue makes a vivid case for the efficacy of concentrating and conserving one's professional energies, so as to create (in this instance, anyway) a powerful architecture in direct response to the limits on that energy.

It is astonishing to realize that all that profoundly important work came out of just eight years in the Brookline *atélier*, with Richardson frequently ill and, apparently, aware of how short a time remained to him. The parallel is striking with Michelangelo, for instance, who reached the threshold of his architectural career when he was 71, and could similarly have divined that the time was short. Both men made powerful, simple drawings and lavished their attention on the building itself with an altogether different budgeting of energy from, say, Paul Rudolph, who, endowed with extraordinary stamina, an early start, and the expectation of a long career, could afford to lavish his attention on dazzlingly complex drawings. I kept hearing, as I read O'Gorman's pages, the voice of Jean Labatut teaching at Princeton, continually urging

The ceiling and tower of Trinity Church (above)
A sketch for an unidentified house, by H. H. Richardson (opposite)

"ze maximum effect wiz ze minimum of means," and I wonder if that problem
— of parlaying a limited amount of energy into a large and influential body of
work — is not really the central problem of the professional practitioner.

The conservation of energy, which this book (it seems to me) is about, has
to start from a person, and the wonder is how a set of tiny Richardson sketches,
often done in a sickbed, had the power to summon from his associates contract
drawings which produced, with Richardson's "constant criticism" and "final
oversight," the "massive and simple"[6] buildings that have provided the image
for a whole age. The medium itself provides a clue: the drawings were developed
in pencil, the firm (for the moment) decisions overlaid in a decisive, thick pen
line. The very technique banished the likelihood that the finicky, crocketed
silhouettes of some of Richardson's older contemporaries would appear. It
also militated against the possibility that the sharp-edged lithic curves which
give so much power to the work of Frank Furness would be a part of the Richardson idiom.

But I confess I still don't see how he did it, even though the drawings show
such a careful conservation of the designer's energy, and such clear concentration on the massive and simple. The number of buildings, from Boston to
Chicago and beyond, that had to be travelled to (by train) and fought over and
charmed into being (even though his charm was the wonder of his contemporaries) is staggering. That it was done by one sick man during those eight re-

172

Main door Da Vinci

Screen with ing

markable Brookline years, even given the extraordinarily highly controlled discipline of his design, is almost incredible.

Hitchcock, looking forty years ago at why Richardson's presence was so commanding — and so enduring — called him Modern. It seems to me more helpful, forty years later, to think of him rather as the quintessential full-time architectural professional, the undisputed leader of a complicated team that accomplishes things (the building of buildings of lasting power) with a beautiful economy of effort and a knowledge of how to be effective — driven by ambition, to be sure, but led on by a vision of how things have to be.

C.M.

Envoy

Architecture proceeds by indirection toward its goal of making a place, a many-dimensioned creation responsive to the perceptual spaces of the human mind. It begins with the careful assembly of a limited number of materials of limited properties and dimensions, but the useful product is not the assembly itself. Instead it is something else, a piece of space, marked off from the rest and given dimensions of length and breadth and height and time and place, and connotations out of our perceptions, dreams, visions, and memories.

No slide show, no movie, no book can do more than to hint at the experience of architecture — the surprise of the sun breaking through and shining on a shadowed world, or the thrill of a sudden breeze wafted out of what might be the infinite, or the smell of garlic or of orange blossoms. Nothing short of being there can recreate the revelation that comes at the Athenian Propylaea after the long, hot climb up the slope, a wonder that is composed as much of our imaginary connection with Pericles speaking there as with the perfection of the marble shapes themselves. These are the dimensions of magic, born of our lifelong excitement at the miracle of standing erect, and of our need to establish a territory, and of the rich conglomeration of our experiences and our imaginations.

Yet architecture begins with the simple assembly of physical things, which can, by the way they are put together, begin to embody the dimensions of magic — just as, in a poem, simple words are joined in an orderly way to rhyme and scan, and then, by their assembly, to do a great deal more. Remember that in poetry there are many kinds of poems — sonnets, lyrics, dirges, rounds, limericks (and, yes, even heroic verse). So buildings speak to us in many voices— soft and loud, sober and silly, important and modest. Blessed, especially, are the modest, for they will shortly cover the earth.

Reference Notes

Dimensions

1 Susanne K. Langer, *Feeling and Form*
(New York, Charles Scribner's Sons, 1953),
p. 95.

Space

1 Susanne K. Langer, *Feeling and Form* (New
York, Charles Scribner's Sons, 1953), p. 94.

2 Camillo Sitte, translated by Charles T. Stewart,
The Art of Building Cities (New York,
Reinhold Publishing Corp., 1945).

3 Siegfried Giedion, *Space, Time and
Architecture*, 5th edition (Cambridge, Mass.,
Harvard University Press, 1967).

4 C. A. Doxiadis, translated by Jaqueline
Tyrwhitt, *Architectural Space in Ancient
Greece* (Cambridge, Mass., The MIT Press,
1972).

Shape

1 Andrea Palladio, *The Four Books of
Architecture* (New York, Dover Publications,
1965).

2 Charles Moore, Gerald Allen, Donlyn Lyndon,
The Place of Houses (New York, Holt,
Rinehart and Winston, 1974), p. 143

St. Thomas Church

1 H. L. Bottomley, "The Story of St. Thomas
Church," *Architectural Record*, 35, 2
(February, 1914), 101-31; "A Detail of
Construction," p. 173.

2 Ralph Adams Cram, *Church Buildings*
(Boston, Small, Maynard & Company, 1899),
p. 85.

3 *St. Thomas Church* (New York, privately
printed, 1965), p. 5.

4 Douglass Shand Tucci, *Ralph Adams Cram:
American Medievalist* (Boston, Boston Public
Library, 1975), pp. 30, 35.

Action Architecture

1 Charles Moore, Gerald Allen, Donlyn Lyndon,
The Place of Houses (New York, Holt,
Rinehart and Winston, 1974), pp. 19-30.

2 José Ortega y Gasset, *The Revolt of the Masses*
(New York, W. W. Norton, 1932), pp. 151-52.

Inclusive and Exclusive

1 An earlier version of this essay was entitled
"Plug It in, Rameses, and See if It Lights Up:
Because We Aren't Going to Keep It Unless It

Works;" see *Perspecta 11* (New Haven, The
Yale School of Architecture, 1967), pp. 32-43.

2 Robert Venturi, *Complexity and Contradiction
in Architecture* (New York, The Museum of
Modern Art, 1966).

Hadrian's Villa

1 Eleanor Clark, *Rome and a Villa* (Garden
City, New York, Country Life Press, 1950),
p. 143.

2 Spartian, translated by William Maude, *The
Life of the Emperor Hadrian* (New York,
Cambridge Encyclopedia Co., 1900), p. 23.

3 E. Baldwin Smith, *Architectural Symbolism of
Imperial Rome and the Middle Ages*
(Princeton, Princeton University Press, 1956),
pp. 145-47.

4 Clark, p. 144.

5 Spartian, p. 23.

6 Marguerite Yourcenar, translated by Grace
Frick, *Memoirs of Hadrian* (Farrar, Strauss
and Young, 1954).

7 Strabo, translated by H. C. Hamilton, *The
Geography of Strabo* (London, George Bell &
Sons, 1887), pp. 3, 238.

Likenesses

1 Lewis Mumford, "The Sky Line: Mr.
Rockefeller's Center," *The New Yorker*, 9
(December 23, 1933), pp. 29-30.

2 Robert Venturi, *Complexity and Contradiction
in Architecture* (New York, The Museum of
Modern Art, 1966), p. 133.

3 Jonathan Barnett, *Urban Design as Public
Policy* (New York, Architectural Record Books,
1974), pp. 41-42.

You Have to Pay for the Public Life

1 José Ortega y Gasset, *The Revolt of the Masses*
(New York, W. W. Norton, 1932), pp. 151, 152.

Discrimination in Housing Design

1 Vincent Scully, Jr., *Louis I. Kahn* (New York,
George Braziller, 1962), p. 120.

2 Robert Venturi, *Complexity and Contradiction
in Architecture* (New York, The Museum of
Modern Art, 1966), p. 11.

3 Charles Moore, Gerald Allen, Donlyn Lyndon,
The Place of Houses (New York, Holt,
Rinehart and Winston, 1974), pp. 82, 108-109.

Southernness

1 Lewis Mumford, *The South in Architecture* (New York, Da Capo Press, 1967).

2 Edmund N. Bacon, *The Design of Cities* (New York, The Viking Press, 1974), pp. 216-17.

3 Vincent Scully, *American Architecture and Urbanism* (New York, Frederick A. Praeger, 1969).

Schindler and Richardson

1 David Gebhard, *Schindler* (New York, The Viking Press, 1972).

2 Moshe Safdie, *Beyond Habitat* (Cambridge, Mass., The MIT Press, 1970).

3 James F. O'Gorman, editor, *H. H. Richardson and his Office: Selected Drawings* (Boston, David R. Godine, 1974).

4 Mariana Griswold Van Rensselaer, *Henry Hobson Richardson and His Works* (New York, Dover Publications, 1969).

5 Henry-Russell Hitchcock, *The Architecture of H. H. Richardson and His Times* (Cambridge, Mass., The MIT Press, 1966).

6 Van Rensselaer, p. 123.

Illustration Credits

Gerald Allen
Pages 30, 34, 35, 37 left & right, 39, 42, 43, 44 right, 45, 47 top, 99 right & left, top & bottom, 103, 116, 132, 133 top & bottom right, 134, 135 top, center left & bottom right, 136 left & right, 141, 142, 147 left & right, 149, 150 left, 152 bottom, 154, 155 bottom, 156.

Architectural Record
Pages 33 left & right, 36.

Morley Baer
Page 127.

Beinecke Library, Yale University
Pages 86, 88.

Gunnar Birkerts and Associates
Pages 63, 64 top, 67.

Paul David Birnbaum
Pages 26, 32, 49, 50, 171, 172.

Melinda Blauvelt
Page 47 bottom.

E. Braun
Page 75 top and bottom.

Camera Arts Studio
Page 164 top left.

Centro Internationale di Studi di Architettura A. Palladio
Page 5.

George Cserna
Page 163.

Environmental Communications
Pages 57, 129.

Esherick Homsey Dodge and Davis
Page 77 right.

Federal Reserve Bank of Minneapolis
Pages 64 bottom, 69.

Roy Flamm
Pages 76, 77 top & bottom left, 78, 126.

Joshua Freiwald
Pages 73, 74.

Douglas Gillespie
Page 164 bottom left.

Gwathmey Siegel Architects
Pages 137, 138, 139.

Harr, Hedrich-Blessing
Page 62.

William Hersey
Pages 144, 145, 146, 148, 150 right, 151, 152 top, 153, 155 top.

Houghton Library, Harvard University
Page 173.

Steven Izenour
Page 58.

Heinz Kahler
Pages 83, 90, 91.

Kathleen Kershaw
Pages 72, 125.

Balthazar Korab
Pages 65, 66, 68, 70, 158, 159, 161, 162, 165.

Library of Congress
Page ii.

William McDonald
Pages 82, 87, 89, 92, 93.

McGraw-Hill
Page 102.

MIT Press
Pages 8, 9.

Charles Moore
Pages 46 left & right, 48 left, center & right, 60 right & left, 108, 111, 114, 118, 119, 123, 130.

Michael Moose
Page 59.

Wade Perry
Page 140.

Perspecta
Pages 52, 53, 55, 56 left & right.

Rockefeller Center
Pages viii, 96, 97, 98, 100.

Julius Schulman
Pages 168, 169.

Louis Schwartz
Page 150.

Shepley, Bulfinch, Richardson, and Abbott
Page 170.

Carl Smith
Pages 110, 112, 113, 115 right, 120 left & right, 121.

A. F. Sozio
Page 38.

George Stille
Page 160.

Bruce Torrence Historical Collection
Page 117.

John Veltri
Page 101.

Woollen Associates
Page 164 right,

Index